MW00639443

"Filled with meaningful rhythms, ⸻ ⸻ ⸻ ments, *Comfort and Joy* meets us in t⸻ ⸻ ⸻ cozy companion slows the tempo, steadying our hearts for the abundance of Christmas and the promised arrival of Emmanuel."
—**SHANNAN MARTIN**, author of *Start with Hello* and *The Ministry of Ordinary Places*

"*Comfort and Joy* is much more than 'readings and practices for Advent.' It's a celebration of family and friendship and stories of days past and present, with reflections on Scripture, recipes, poetry, and prayers of blessing that start with Advent and take us through Christmas all the way to Epiphany. Reading this book was a gift to me, and I'm happy to recommend it as a gift of grace for the Advent and Christmas season."
—**APRIL YAMASAKI**, pastor and author of *Sacred Pauses* and *Four Gifts*

"If you're anything like me, you want to prepare well for the coming of Jesus during the season of Advent. And—if you're like me—you know that everything else gets in the way. The authors of *Comfort and Joy* are the guides I need. They know what my life is like. Living with the same challenges of being human that I face, their words gently usher me out of the chaos and into what's holy."
—**MARGOT STARBUCK**, author of *Small Things with Great Love*

"*Comfort and Joy* is the perfect Advent devotional for busy readers who yearn to experience anew the wonder and joy of Christmas. Through a weekly rhythm of reflections and questions, practices and prayers, readings and recipes, Sherah-Leigh Gerber and Gwen Lantz guide our hearts and minds into a fresh encounter with the profound miracle of Jesus' birth—God with us. Beautifully written, with relatable stories from two down-to-earth authors, *Comfort and Joy* is one of those rare books I plan to reread year after year."
—**JASON PORTERFIELD**, author of *Fight Like Jesus*

"In the rush and frenzy of the Christmas season, *Comfort and Joy* is a breath of fresh air that helps readers pause and ground themselves in the joy, goodness, and blessings of the season. This is a delightful book of story, reflection, and practical rhythms for individuals, families, and churches!"
—**BRENDA L. YODER**, author of *Uncomplicated*

Comfort & Joy

READINGS & PRACTICES for ADVENT

Sherah-Leigh Gerber & Gwen Lantz

HERALD PRESS

Harrisonburg, Virginia

Herald Press
PO Box 866, Harrisonburg, Virginia 22803
www.HeraldPress.com

Library of Congress Cataloging-in-Publication Data
Names: Gerber, Sherah-Leigh, author. | Lantz, Gwen, author.
Title: Comfort and joy : readings and practices for Advent / Sherah-Leigh Gerber
   and Gwen Lantz.
Description: Harrisonburg, Virginia : Herald Press, [2024] | Includes bibliographical
   references.
Identifiers: LCCN 2024011123 (print) | LCCN 2024011124 (ebook) | ISBN
   9781513813271 (paperback) | ISBN 9781513813288 (ebooks)
Subjects: LCSH: Advent—Prayers and devotions. | BISAC: RELIGION / Christian Living
   / Devotional Journal | RELIGION / Christian Living / Spiritual Growth
Classification: LCC BX2170.A4 G48 2024 (print) | LCC BX2170.A4 (ebook) |
   DDC 242/.332—dc23/eng/20240513
LC record available at https://lccn.loc.gov/2024011123
LC ebook record available at https://lccn.loc.gov/2024011124

Study guides are available for many Herald Press titles at www.HeraldPress.com.

COMFORT AND JOY
© 2024 by Herald Press, Harrisonburg, Virginia, 22803. 800-245-7894.
All rights reserved.
Library of Congress Control Number: 1234567890
International Standard Book Number: 978-1-5138-1327-1 (paperback);
   978-1-5138-1328-8 (ebook)

Printed in United States of America
Cover and interior design by Merrill Miller
Illustrations adapted from Marina/GettyImages

All rights reserved. This publication may not be reproduced, stored in a retrieval system, or transmitted in whole or in part, in any form, by any means, electronic, mechanical, photo-copying, recording or otherwise without prior permission of the copyright owners.

   Scripture quotations are from the New Revised Standard Version Updated Edition. Copyright © 2021 National Council of Churches of Christ in the United States of America. Used by permission. All rights reserved worldwide.

28 27 26 25 24   10 9 8 7 6 5 4 3 2 1

For our mothers and grandmothers,
who passed on their faith and creativity despite adversity.
And for our families, who have shown us the sacred in the ordinary.

Contents

Introduction

GWEN

One of my earliest holiday memories is of my family's annual Christmas Day trip to Pennsylvania from our Virginia home in the Shenandoah Valley. Getting up early enough to open gifts before we set out down the interstate, we made the four-hour drive, arriving in time for the big Christmas dinner.

My grandparents were Amish, so in some ways the trip was a bit like traveling into another time. I was, in reality, sojourning to another culture. We started in the rural, southern countryside, where we were the only Stoltzfus in the phonebook, and arrived in a community where the same last name took up pages and pages.

As we passed through my grandparents' door each year, we were greeted with kisses and handshakes all around the room. Women, in particular, were clothed differently, wearing cape dresses and coverings on their heads. My mother, sister, and I all wore dresses on that day to smooth the relational rough spots as these two cultures interacted within the same extended family.

Even though the interactions were sometimes complicated, one thing was certain—there was a place for everyone at my grandmother's table. Sitting together to share a meal is deeply significant in Amish culture. In some traditions, when a person leaves the Amish community, as my father had done, they are no longer permitted to dine at the same table with their former community members. For my grandmother, divided card tables throughout the house would not do. Just one very long table. As the family grew, the long table moved to a basement room and became several long tables fully extended, connected one after the other and dressed in tablecloths, with china plates at *every* seat.

This specially prepared table and the generous meal enjoyed there is symbolic of the invitation God has extended to us and our communities. The table is long and there is space for each of us to sit down and join in the celebration. In this season of Advent, we prepare to participate in Christmas activities and we also celebrate the joyful reality of God's presence on earth in Jesus—God with us. As you journey through Advent and on into Christmastide this year, our hope is that you will experience the same kind of warm welcome, beauty, and delight that I did when I entered the door of my grandparent's house.

About Us

A few years ago, I was scrolling the internet looking for a Christian devotional for the Advent season. I didn't want long theological essays or lists of things I should do to experience the perfect holiday season. I wasn't looking for a family devotional or activities for my children. I was longing to nurture my own spirit, despite—or maybe in the midst of—the early morning rush, the crush of events that fill the holiday season, and the daily reality of work and laundry. I know too well how easy it can be to disappear into the chaos and activity of a busy life. I wanted something to help me approach the holiday season with a different set of priorities.

That fruitless search planted the seed to create what I was longing for, and the following spring I approached my friend and fellow writer, Sherah-Leigh, with the idea of creating a blog geared to women who want meaningful and accessible reflections to help them connect with God, especially around seasonal themes. What began as a devotional blog project in the months before the global COVID-19 pandemic upended life as we knew it has not only been a creative outlet for us, but also a place of spiritual nurture and encouragement for folks in many places and stages of life.

Our writing at the blog *Some Comfort and Joy* focuses on our everyday lives. It is specific in that we write about our family experiences, conversations with friends, and work interactions. And it is universal as it creates connections around themes that have resonated with others and their own individual life experiences.

The unique invitation to reflection and practice that we have shared over the past few years in our *Some Comfort and Joy* community has been such a gift. We love to have a place to offer our learning, questions, and rhythms that have encouraged our faith journeys as we navigate the challenges of life. Though we now write from different parts of the United States instead of opposite ends of town, we continue to be passionate about sharing the glimpses of the holy in our ordinary lives, and we're delighted for you to join us in making space and seeing goodness anew in the everyday.

The book you now hold is a collaboration between two friends. It is a resource for those longing to connect with God this Advent and Christmas season. It isn't about adding to your list of things that must be accomplished or a how-to manual for taming holiday stresses. Through simple practices and thoughtful prompts you are invited to be intentional in taking time to reflect and celebrate. Life isn't always easy, especially during the holiday season, but there are many beautiful moments to be created and remembered.

Without a doubt, God is ever present as we journey toward the celebration of the birth of Christ. May we have open hearts to learn, reflect, and grow this Advent and Christmas season.

About This Book

Advent is the start of the liturgical year in the broader Christian tradition. Growing up in Mennonite congregations, we did not always celebrate and closely follow the church seasons of Advent and Lent, but we have grown to find these to be very meaningful times of preparation and nurture in our lives.

Expectation and anticipation are the points of focus for Advent, the four weeks leading up to celebrating Christmas. On December 25, we celebrate the incarnation, the birth of Jesus. This marks the start of the twelve days of Christmas, culminating in Epiphany (referred to as Old Christmas in Amish communities), where we recognize the gifts of the magi.

And so this book offers reflections, prompts, invitations, and blessings to nurture your soul through Advent and into Christmastide. Each week is focused around a theme drawn from the scripture texts following *A Women's Lectionary for the Whole Church* by Wilda C. Gafney.[1] The lectionary is a resource for the church that moves through the Bible in a three-year cycle. Each calendar year is organized around the seasons of the church year (Advent, Christmas, and Epiphany; Lent and Easter; Pentecost; and Ordinary Time). Many churches use this rhythm for worship planning, and it can help us to engage in special holy times, like Advent. We chose to use Gafney's resource as the anchor point for our devotional because we value and appreciate how she centers the stories of women. In a season where we hear what are likely familiar stories, choosing to honor the perspectives and voices that are often marginalized offers fresh insights and connections with the biblical stories and our own life experiences.

While our devotional guide has a repeating weekly rhythm to move us through the six-week liturgical church seasons of Advent, Christmas, and Epiphany, you may choose to use this as a daily or weekly guide starting after American Thanksgiving, on the first Sunday of Advent, or at the beginning of December.

We hope each person will be able to engage *Comfort and Joy* in unique ways that reflect the rhythms of your own life, so the entries are intentionally labeled by week and theme instead of by day. Perhaps you will choose to adopt a sabbath practice of reading each week's offerings on your day of rest or worship. If your routine allows, you could take time to connect with two of the offerings on each of the weekdays or read one piece per day, adding in the poem, scripture, and blessing on the last day of your week. You may even decide to select a few pages based on your day or week. However you choose to engage, there is no wrong way to experience the invitation to deeper wonder!

Methods for spiritual reflection and practice are as varied as we are as individuals. Some people find that baking a new cookie recipe is a way to still their mind, relax, and reflect. Others don't want to *do* anything, instead preferring to sit in quiet reflection. Perhaps taking a poignant thought from one of the reflections and holding that idea for the week would be the perfect spiritual discipline for you this Advent and Christmas season. There are many ways to commune with God in our daily lives, and we hope you will feel free to engage with the suggested practices that most resonate with you during this season.

Each week is comprised of the following elements:

Poems offer a way to engage, often at an emotive level, in the beauty and the challenges of the holiday season. We begin with a poem as a way of inviting a reflective spirit and encouraging a gentle pause.

Theme Reflections are focused on an idea carried through the week. Each of the six weeks of Advent and Christmastide offers a new topic to consider. These personal essays are drawn from our friendship and experiences in everyday life. Each week includes a reflection from each author. One occurs after the poem at the beginning of the week. The second reflection precedes the closing blessing of the week.

The **Practices of Joy** are an invitation to action. These are opportunities to integrate the weekly themes into your daily life. Each practice has a variety of choices for application and often suggests ways to tackle everyday tasks with a new perspective.

Lectionary Texts appear each week and follow Wilda C. Gafney's *Women's Lectionary for the Whole Church (Year W)*. All scripture references are from the New Revised Standard Version Updated Edition.

The **Words of Comfort** are reflections connecting the theme for the week and the scripture text as a starting point for deeper consideration. The words of comfort follow a more traditional devotional format. Each opens with a scripture and closes with a simple prayer. As with the theme reflections, each week contains a word of comfort from each of us.

We have included **Recipes** that evoke the holiday season, drawn from our Mennonite and Amish heritages and family traditions, which we hope will not only prompt connections to your own upbringing but also offer new savory and sweet foods to add to your repertoire. We have intentionally placed our recipes and their accompanying stories in the middle of the week's offerings as an acknowledgment that food is an essential part of our ordinary lives and that God meets us there, in the midst of the mundane.

Each **Pause for Reflection** provides questions connected to the scripture text and theme for contemplation. While we find writing to be a meaningful spiritual discipline that slows down our whirring minds and helps us arrive at new understandings about ourselves and our faith, we recognize that there are a variety of ways to respond. You may choose to simply consider the questions in your mind, process verbally with a friend, type your thoughts in a notes app, or write in your journal.

Blessings conclude each week and offer encouragement for whatever is next. Sometimes during the busy holiday season that "next" may just mean the coming moment. This prayerful conclusion provides a chance for you to take a deep breath and soak in God's promises.

Invitation to Advent

SHERAH-LEIGH

Scripture opens with the story of creation. Out of chaos, God lovingly brings order and beauty. God creates rhythms. God gives light and dark, day and night. God forms humanity from the dust of the earth and enlivens us with the Spirit. God created humankind in the divine image, within and for community. From the very beginning God was with humankind and declared that it was good.

In this Genesis story of creation and community, we learn of broken relationships and how they impact the divine connection. For Adam and Eve, it is not that God cannot bear to see them, but that their own shame and guilt, their newfound knowledge, now separates them from God.

Yet God continues to show up. God pursues them. "Where are you?" God calls.

God continues to call and collect this group of people who eventually wander in the wilderness, who make idols, who beg for kings, who disregard the words of the prophets. And then God decides, much as it was in the very beginning, that it is not good for God's people to be alone in this way.

So, God comes to God's people. God comes to humankind in the flesh, taking on human form—Emmanuel.

Jesus came, and God was with us. It's the Advent story woven into the grand story of God. God created. God walked with Adam and Eve. God connected with the people in the tabernacle and then the temple. God took on flesh and walked among us, and when that physical, earthly presence ended in crucifixion, the veil in the Most Holy Place was torn. There was no longer separation between God and God's people.

God is loudly proclaiming: *I have always been present. I have always been near. I am here. I am with you.*

No matter how you are approaching this Advent season, there is good news. The words of scripture, written long ago, demonstrate again and again that God is at work. God is present. God is always surprising God's people by moving and making something new.

In the midst of a weary world and fragile hope, we come to this season of preparation and celebration to be reminded of this truth. We engage in these reflective practices so we, too, can notice anew that God is with us, in the beauty of the ordinary and in the sacred extraordinary of Advent and Christmastide.

It is our hope and prayer that our journey together in this season will bring you some comfort and joy.

WEEK I

Preparation

Advent Questions

SHERAH-LEIGH

When an angel appears there is fear.
Do you feel it?
Do not be afraid!

When the announcement is made there is wondering.
How can this be?
Let it be with me.

When the invitation is accepted there is waiting.
Can you stand it?
Blessed is she!

Reluctant Preparation

GWEN

Composting and preparing the soil before planting a garden is essential if you want thriving plants later in the year. That's what my sister, Karla, will tell you. She is an organic gardener, and wherever she lives, beautiful flower gardens soon bloom. Karla's undergraduate degree in international agriculture as well as a master of divinity degree allow her to wax eloquent about the beauty of dark, rich soil filled with micronutrients and earthworms. She has preached whole sermons on the spiritual symbolism of compost. On the practical side, there is plenty I've learned from her about how to compost well. Not the least of which is if you want a beautiful, bountiful garden, you need rich soil. And soil can be amended—even dried out, used up soil can be brought back to life with some care and preparation.

You'd think that I would take a page from my sister's sermon and spend more time preparing the soil each fall and spring in my vegetable garden. But looking ahead hasn't always been my strong suit, and doubly so for spiritual matters. It's not that I'm unorganized. It's just that I often commit to more than I can actually, humanly do. No time of year brings out this tendency in me quite like Christmas. With the added time commitments of attending school concerts, hosting extra special events and family, decorating, and preparing food, it is easy to get overwhelmed.

Preparation, both physical and spiritual, can be tricky for me as a person who prefers to live in the moment. While I long to have the details of future events in place, securing them sometimes eludes me as I solve life's immediate problems instead. When I arrive at the event, I can find myself disappointed in the details and outcomes I didn't account for. In the Christmas season, that can be compounded by the relational angst that comes from socializing with people I don't see frequently, often in large gatherings. But even more importantly, those physical preparations can distract from the important work of preparing my heart during Advent.

Advent is a season centered around preparation. As a time to prepare our hearts and minds to celebrate Christ's coming, the Advent season invites us to reflect and wait. Hopefully this creates space in our lives for us to recognize God at work—not only long ago, but today. Just as those in the first century waited for a Messiah (Mary and Joseph included), we wait and prepare to celebrate the reality of Jesus' birth and the promise of his second coming as well.

And yet too often our experience of Advent is defined by the stress of preparing for the outward signs and symbols of the holiday season. It *is* easy to get caught up in all the events, the decorating and shopping for presents, the general hubbub.

And the expectations! Many of us carry around (okay, drag from room to room) not only our own hopes for experiencing holiday joy, but also the expectations of our children, spouses, or extended families. Additionally, we carry the weight of expectations of the communities around us, like church Advent and Christmas events, special concerts, and parties in our children and grandchildren's lives.

It may be shocking to admit as someone who's now writing an Advent devotional, but I have been known to say, "I don't even like the holidays. Can we just skip them?" How sad is that? And those words do not reflect how I actually want to feel.

While I may not excel at preparation, one of Sherah-Leigh's many strengths is her ability to anticipate what is coming down the road and thoughtfully prepare. From my friendship with Sherah-Leigh I have learned so much about the benefits of intentional spiritual preparation and reflection. Sometimes we grow through life's tough, unexpected experiences, and I certainly have. But I have learned from my friend that we can grow with purpose and thoughtfulness as well.

So, I make the lists and color code my calendar all in an effort to control the unfolding of the Christmas season, and I also allow myself to focus on what matters most in this season. Because I can get overwhelmed with stress during the holidays, heart preparation has been an area of growth for me. Perhaps I have developed some strategies to better manage the activities over the years, but that isn't the heart of Advent. At some point I realized that the real preparation I needed was to create space for reflection and to intentionally look for holy experiences in my everyday life. This isn't achieved by making a simple list or even a complicated, color-coded one. It is a more vulnerable choice—to make time for spiritual reflection and expect God to meet me there.

Preparation, then, is the perfect focus for this first week of reflections and practices. In Advent we prepare our hearts so that the outward signs of the season become acts of kindness and creativity instead of a frustrating list of seasonal to-dos. We can make room in our lives so that when Christ arrives, we are ready to notice and celebrate.

We'll mess up and try again. Mistakes and fresh starts are allowed! Thanks to Karla and Sherah-Leigh, I am reminded that it is good to prepare—not just our calendars, but also our hearts—for this season of spiritual waiting and watching for God's work in our lives. Just like depleted soil can be restored, so too can our souls.

Rushing from one activity to the next will not get you where you want to be in these coming weeks. Instead, with anticipation and intention, grab your mug of something warm and comforting, and join us on this journey through Advent with a spirit of preparation. Give yourself permission to open your heart to the movement of God's Spirit, especially if you feel nudged toward something that isn't on the list. May you prepare yourself so that holy, unexpected experiences will blossom in your home this Advent and Christmas, just like the flowers in my sister's garden.

Gathering Evergreens

SHERAH-LEIGH

Marking the time leading up to Christmas is one way we prepare our hearts and pay attention to the invitations and opportunities that Advent holds. In the northern hemisphere, this time is also marked by the growing darkness. The hours of daylight diminish as the calendar moves closer to Christmas. This is perhaps one reason candles have become such an important symbol in Advent celebrations across time and cultures.

Growing up, an Advent wreath served as my family's dining table centerpiece for the month of December. Some years ago, I started a new tradition with my own family when I acquired an Advent spiral, a flat wooden coil with notches for twenty-four candles. Through the season, the Advent spiral remains on our kitchen table, and each day we move the candle a spot inward to mark the nearing of Christmas.

The Advent wreath began as a Lutheran tradition in Germany: four candles surround a fifth candle known as the "Christ candle," and the wreath is one way Christians have marked the time leading up to Christmas. Highly symbolic, the candles (light), the circular form of a wreath (everlasting), and the use of evergreens (eternal life) are all reminders of the hope of Christ's birth celebrated at Christmas.

Take some time to prepare your own Advent arrangement. Consider what you already own that you could gather to display. You may choose to use the traditional form of the wreath, to fill a bowl with pinecones, or to create a centerpiece of pine branches and boughs. Perhaps you'd even like to try using an Advent spiral. If you don't have appropriate items within your current seasonal decor, consider heading outside and collecting pieces from nature to use.

Whether a centerpiece for your dining table, a topper for your fireplace mantle, or an arrangement on a coffee table, you can use this as a reminder throughout the coming weeks of the promise of Advent: *a light shines in the darkness and the darkness will not overcome it* (see John 1:5).

Luke 1:26–38

In the sixth month the angel Gabriel was sent by God to a town in Galilee called Nazareth, to a virgin engaged to a man whose name was Joseph, of the house of David. The virgin's name was Mary.

And he came to her and said, "Greetings, favored one! The Lord is with you."

But she was much perplexed by his words and pondered what sort of greeting this might be. The angel said to her, "Do not be afraid, Mary, for you have found favor with God. And now, you will conceive in your womb and bear a son, and you will name him Jesus. He will be great and will be called the Son of the Most High, and the Lord God will give to him the throne of his ancestor David. He will reign over the house of Jacob forever, and of his kingdom there will be no end."

Mary said to the angel, "How can this be, since I am a virgin?"

The angel said to her, "The Holy Spirit will come upon you, and the power of the Most High will overshadow you; therefore the child to be born will be holy; he will be called Son of God. And now, your relative Elizabeth in her old age has also conceived a son, and this is the sixth month for her who was said to be barren. For nothing will be impossible with God."

Then Mary said, "Here am I, the servant of the Lord; let it be with me according to your word."

Then the angel departed from her.

Mary's Miracle

GWEN

*"For nothing will be impossible with God." Then Mary said,
"Here am I, the servant of the Lord; let it be with me according
to your word." Then the angel departed from her.*
—LUKE 1:37–38

In Advent, time itself can seem suspended for a bit as we recall and re-inhabit the many traditions that have been passed down in our families and communities. We remember the celebrations of our childhood and often carefully plan our own holiday gatherings. We hang the lights, bake the cookies, buy the gifts, and send out the invitations. We are surrounded by all that has gone before us as we celebrate the holidays. We have expectations of how we will experience the season.

Mary was part of her own community and faith tradition. When the angel appeared to Mary, she was planning a wedding. She most certainly had a few expectations of the months ahead of her. Carrying the baby of the Most High God wasn't part of her original plan.

And yet in that sudden moment, the angel's announcement rearranges her agenda. "How can this be?" Mary asked the angel, according to the account in Luke. Although Luke doesn't tell us whether everything fell into place for Mary after the visit from the angel, I think it is realistic to assume that Mary experienced difficulties along the way as her unexpected pregnancy became obvious to her community.

Life can feel like that in today's modern world as well. While we may not have experienced anything quite like Mary's unique situation, many of us know what it's like to confront unmet expectations. Sometimes life's surprises are a mix of good and bad. And sometimes the unexpected leaves us feeling hopeless. A cancer diagnosis, a divorce, new responsibilities caring for loved ones, children who clamor for extra time and attention, friendship conflicts and financial instability—the unexpected can arrive in many ways. And when it does, we are left wondering, not unlike Mary, *how can this be?*

Mary, while surprised and uncertain at first, ultimately decides to believe that God can work miracles. Some days I find that choice just as amazing as the virgin birth. The angel didn't promise her a future with no hardship, but Gabriel did bring news of a miracle. This story reminds us that God often does amazing things *when* we least expect it. Quite frequently, God does not do *what* we were expecting either.

During Advent, we wait with anticipation. And along with Mary, we marvel at the message from angel Gabriel, that with God all things are possible.

God, we want to be prepared for all the planned events of the Advent season. Help us also to be open to the unexpected so we won't overlook your miracles when they arrive. Amen.

Great-Grandma's Soft Sugar Cookies

GWEN

My mother, Catherine Ramer Stoltzfus, has taught me so much about preparation. When company visited during my childhood, she made lists, cleaned rooms, and created menus with care. Sometimes we spent our days planting flower seeds around the edge of the garden, together laying the groundwork for a beautiful rainbow border in the summer months to follow. Other days she taught me about the beauty that could be created by adding fresh parsley sprigs to a platter of roasted turkey. For my mother, preparation often involved thinking ahead to the needs and enjoyment of others around her, and it brought her personal joy and satisfaction to bring her plans to reality and see other people delight in those creations.

As an adult, I have appreciated listening to stories about how my conservative Mennonite grandmother took great care to prepare an overflowing table for her guests as well—her tiered fruit platters topped with divinity fudge (see bonus recipe for Chocolate Divinity Candy on page 153) at Christmas time are legendary in my mom's family. In the Mennonite culture, where lavish holiday gifts were often unaffordable or considered worldly, creating and serving a delicious holiday meal was one way women expressed love to their family. Elaborate plates of cookies and bright red cranberry salad were not just practical but a way to express creativity.

This soft, drop sugar cookie brings happy memories of my mother's baking and holiday preparations. It is also one of my children's favorite cookie recipes. Many years before they or even I ever tasted one, my mother, as a farm girl, made hundreds of these sugar cookies each week for her family's booth at the local market. The recipe has now been passed down in our family at least from as far back as my great-grandmother.

During our first Christmas in the COVID-19 pandemic, when we couldn't gather as an extended family, my siblings and I, each in our own kitchens, made these sugar cookies together over Zoom with my mom giving us instructions.

Among the various delights on the Christmas cookie plate, these cookies in particular speak to me of generations of family tradition and preparation. I hope they will bring to mind your own family traditions as you enjoy these tender and sweet delights.

GREAT-GRANDMA'S SOFT SUGAR COOKIES

Ingredients

3 cups brown sugar
1 cup lard*
5 eggs
3 teaspoons vanilla
1 cup sour milk
1 teaspoon baking soda
2 teaspoons baking powder
4 to 5 cups all-purpose flour
Cinnamon sugar or colored sprinkles (optional topping)

*1¼ cups (2½ sticks) butter can be substituted successfully for lard

Method

Preheat the oven to 375°F degrees. Mix brown sugar, lard, eggs, and vanilla in a large bowl. Beat together until smooth.

In a separate bowl, mix together sour milk and baking soda.

Into the large bowl with the original sugar and lard mixture, now add baking powder. Add one cup of flour at a time alternately with the milk mixture.

Take care to add just enough flour so that the mixture holds together. The final mixture should be soft and light in texture. There is a large range in the amount of flour that can be added to the dough. Flour helps to bind the ingredients together and creates a firmer cookie; the more flour added, the denser the cookie will become. However, adding less flour is desirable, since the cookie will have a lighter and sweeter taste. Add as little flour as possible to maintain a plump, soft sugar cookie.

Drop the mixture by large teaspoonfuls onto dark, ungreased baking sheets about two inches apart. Sprinkle with cinnamon sugar or colored sprinkles, if desired. Bake for 6 minutes, or until the cookies are lightly browned and dome-shaped.

It is a good idea to try baking one or two cookies first. If they spread too much or have dark brown, thin edges, add more flour. If the cookies are still spreading after adding more flour, try making them smaller in size. Also, using dark baking sheets helps to prevent spreading and maintain the dome shape.

Yields 8 to 9 dozen cookies

How Can This Be?

SHERAH-LEIGH

Mary said to the angel, "How can this be . . . ?"
—LUKE 1:34

On my journey with infertility, some of the hardest times were during the Christmas season. The emphasis and focus on pregnancy and birth, along with the images of a sweet baby, were painful reflection points. The historical and (at times flawed) theological teachings around barren-ness and birthing were fraught reminders of my own broken dreams and unmet expectations.

Many of us prepare for a particular kind of life, and when we encounter the inevitable twists and turns, the upending of what we envisioned for ourselves, it can be hard to change course and adjust our expectations.

At times, acts of preparation become ways to manage our anxieties about an uncertain future. We do the physical work of getting ready. We take action, busying ourselves to avoid the discomfort that comes with waiting.

But preparation and anticipation in this season are about more than completing chores or wrapping gifts. It's fine, perhaps even necessary, to put up the Christmas tree, initiate gatherings, and plan menus. Yet the invitation to Christians in Advent is to something much richer—we are invited to prepare our hearts and minds to engage spiritually as we anticipate the celebration of Emmanuel, God with us.

The familiar scripture texts recounting the Christmas story remind us that Jesus' incarnation began with upended expectations and unexpected opportunities. While it is vulnerable to be in liminal or in-between space, to be on the threshold, this time of preparation is necessary to get in touch with our hopes and desires. What are you longing for? What questions do you have for God?

The story of God's relationship with humankind begins with God creating out of the chaos and chronicles unmet longings, misunderstandings, and relational conflict. Yet none of this is a surprise to God, who consistently and faithfully reaches out to us. What would it take for you, like Mary, to move from "How can this be?" to "Here I am; let it be!"?

God, at times you surprise us with invitations and a change in course. May I be receptive to the unexpected opportunities this Advent season holds. May I wait with hope and respond in joy. Amen.

Releasing Expectations

GWEN

Spend some time reflecting on your own expectations for the holiday season. Since Advent can be especially busy, finding time for reflection might be challenging. However, carving out at least one time during the week when you can be alone and quiet is a meaningful spiritual practice, no matter what your schedule entails or your personality inclines you to prefer.

Before you reflect, take a few deep breaths and settle your body. When you are focused, think or journal about the following questions:

- What are you expecting from yourself this Advent and Christmas?

- What plans for holiday fun are realistic, and what might be better released either to be pursued in another stage of life or set aside permanently as not worth the time and effort?

- Which expectations are ones you can and want to fulfill?

- What (perhaps unrealized) expectations do you have of your family and friends for the holiday season?

- Have you ever been surprised by an unexpected blessing? What was it? Retell the story in your journal or to a friend to solidify the memory.

Now that you have spent time considering the hopes and expectations you are carrying, invite God's presence into your planning. Consider the people and situations that are difficult for you. Imagine placing them into God's loving embrace. Invite God's grace to be your companion in these days of preparation and anticipation.

Miracle-making God, help us to enter softly into the Advent season you have prepared for us. It is you, after all, who are the miracle maker—not us. Fill our hearts with wonder as we prepare for Christmas. We desire your presence in our homes and in our very selves. God, we don't want to be negligent in our heart preparation. Grant us wisdom as our schedules fill. Mercifully grant that we could, alongside the prophets of old, prepare a clear path, a highway even, for you. That our time and creativity will invite holy moments. And when you arrive unexpectedly, despite all our planning for things to happen on a particular timetable and in a certain way, may we, like Mary, have the courage to believe and welcome you in. Amen.

Good in the Present

SHERAH-LEIGH

My family's first few years back in the Shenandoah Valley after living in another state for five years involved navigating a number of transitions in rather quick succession—two different houses, three new jobs—and we found ourselves needing to make yet another decision about kindergarten registration for our daughter. I wasn't prepared.

Looking back now, I don't know what I was thinking. In all my dreams and ideas about what parenthood would be like, I certainly didn't anticipate how unprepared I would be for what seems like the unending string of decisions, many of which feel weighted with significance.

I consider my thoughtful, logical, detail-oriented mind to be one of my greatest strengths, but the shadow side of (over)thinking is that I begin to believe I can control all the outcomes; somehow, I can perfect the future if I prepare thoroughly enough. In addition to being untrue, this limiting belief also puts a lot of pressure on me as I make each decision. It becomes very easy to lose track of appropriate expectations, personal responsibility, and (perhaps most importantly) proportion of impact.

When Gwen and I attended church together, we weren't more than acquaintances for a few years—different stages of life and such. But when I moved back to Virginia, I kept hearing about this spunky and delightful Gwen from my sister, since they were in a small group together. As I remember it, by the time Gwen and I met over coffee, I had worked myself into quite the tizzy over my daughter's educational future. I was in great distress, in part about the likely struggling state of private Christian colleges fifteen years into the future.

After patiently listening to me ramble on and enumerate my many fears, Gwen said, "The way I have come to see it, you do the best you can for as long as you can. What is the best decision for today? What makes sense for right now, with the information you have and the things that are within your control?"

Her wise and calm response didn't diminish my concerns but helped me to determine what decisions I actually had to make. Her questions brought me to the present moment. What felt overwhelming and unknowable became more manageable as Gwen's counsel caused me to pause and consider simply doing the next right thing, taking the small step before me.

Careful planning and thoughtful preparation for the future have a place in our lives, just as being in the moment is a valuable discipline. The soul work is in finding the balance, living within the tension, embracing the both/and of now and later.

While it may sound simple and obvious, in the pressures and realities of daily life it can be difficult to embrace this way of being. In the same way, a desire to do the *right* thing and to choose the *best* path (also known as the general pull of perfectionism) can distract or even paralyze us from making any decision at all. Being so consumed with concerns about the future can keep us from noticing the blessings of the present and enjoying the good in the now.

This time of year has the potential to feel more sacred, to draw our attention to the holy things around us. However, every day, in its ordinariness and routine, is an invitation to experience God's presence and goodness in and around us. It's about our orientation toward God's work in the world. How are we preparing to engage the responsibilities, connections, and opportunities of each new day?

As you prepare for all that these weeks will hold, spend some time reflecting on how you are as you approach this season. Based on the year you have had, what do you need this holiday season to be? Considering the commitments and limitations of this month, what would be most meaningful for you? Acknowledging the things that are within your control and the information you hold, what is the best thing you can do for your soul in this particular Advent?

We begin the season of Advent focusing on preparation, in the hope that it is a life-giving invitation for your heart and soul. This first week is meant to remind you to make space to reflect on what is most significant for you right now.

Blessing for the Waiting

SHERAH-LEIGH

When the light is dim,
and I wonder . . .
Remind me that you come near;
for I am waiting.

I am expectant.
I am preparing;
for I know you work wonders.

For healing,
for reconciliation,
I am waiting.

You announce mysteries.
You choose the surprising.
You keep hope alive.
You fulfill your promises.

You transform the ordinary.
You make a way when there seems to be none.
And I am waiting.

And so may I not only know,
but also practice believing.
While I am waiting.

WEEK 2

Hope

Hope Haikus

GWEN

seed beneath damp soil
quietly stirs the darkness
hope waits for warmth, sun

a painter's brushstroke
bow hovering over strings
writer's tapping keys

Elizabeth shouts
in her womb, John leaps for joy
Mother Mary sings

Living in the Gap

SHERAH-LEIGH

Clutching our paper cups of hot chocolate peaked with whipped cream, we exchanged a long look. While Gwen and I love to spend time together, our working-mom schedules didn't leave much space for leisurely coffee dates, particularly in the run-up to the holiday season. We were waiting for a few others from the congregation to join us at the local coffee shop; we were meeting to develop with worship response activities for the children of our church in Advent. Before the other participants arrived, we took advantage of the few minutes of time together to touch base. "How are you feeling about the holidays?" I asked hesitantly.

Over the course of our friendship, we have now both lost a parent-in-law. And we have shared many conversations and tears processing our own grief as we also worked to support our spouses and kids in their unique and varied grief journeys. There are many touchpoints where the pain of loss is particularly sharp, but for both of us that first Christmas after the death of a parent-in-law was especially fraught.

The nostalgia and comfort of traditions are part of the allure of the season. But after a major loss, they are also what can feed into the stressful swirl: Sadness around beloved rhythms changing. Grief when generations pass on. Spiking anxiety as we try to perfectly recreate sacred rituals as though nothing has changed while nothing will ever be the same.

In the anthology of resource essays for spiritual directors entitled *Kaleidoscope*, womanist theologian and professor of religion Phillis Isabella Sheppard notes that "sometimes we try to use this season to make up or repair past holiday seasons."[2] She further considers how, in our unreflective and frantic activity and expectations around tradition, we end up repeating the very disappointment we are trying to avoid.

Traditions bind us in all senses of the word! Familiar rituals, habits, and patterns can connect us with our loved ones. But particularly for those of us who are tasked with the work of making the magic happen, traditions can also generate great stress and anxiety if we become stretched too thin or consumed with creating (or recreating) some perfect moment or experience.

Peanut butter blossoms, lemon melt-aways, cranberry-orange slice-and-bakes, and of course, cut-out sugar cookies (iced and sprinkled), were among the more than dozen types of Christmas cookies that my mother-in-law and her friends cranked out on their annual cookie baking day. That didn't include the caramels, peanut clusters, and Wheatie Balls (see bonus recipe on page 162) that were also made, wrapped, and divided among the families.

I grew up in a pastor's family, and we were always gifted so many plates of homemade treats during the holidays that our Christmas traditions and celebrations didn't center specific foods, but were more about rhythms and activities. So it was a delight for me to join the Gerber family through marriage and experience such fun food rituals; I felt honored to be invited to join the circle of women on the sacred baking day following Thanksgiving.

As my mother-in-law's trio of friends graduated the teenage boys who ate through platters of cookies and shifted their celebrations to include their daughters-in-law and grandchildren, the baking tradition continued to change. Holiday gatherings became focused more on individual family groups instead of the extended family. There were fewer major events requiring the trays of baked goods the moms had historically made. Food allergies and preferences from in-laws and grandkids shifted the menu; the list of "must-have" bakes from home shrank to accommodate the generational favorites from other families. The amount of time spent together became shorter and more intense thanks to new travel plans and sharing adult children's vacation days with the "other side" of the family.

I feel the squeeze of the sandwiching of generations myself, and thus I can relate to the challenge to maintain myriad traditions when you are juggling multiple family systems and trying to find ways to create your own family culture. What will my children remember from their childhood festivities, and which things do I want to be hallmarks of our family legacy?

There simply isn't enough time to do everything, and choosing which things to prioritize can feel fraught. Once we had school-aged children, the number of parties and programs scheduled for the last six weeks of the year increased. Advent is a busy time for church staff as well, and blocking out the calendar space to bake a wide variety of treats in the midst of double-booked days felt like one more to-do rather than a nostalgic touchpoint.

Recognizing that our current family traditions didn't need to be replicas of our childhood rituals in order to be meaningful was a significant relief. Taking time to be intentional and thoughtful about what Advent and Christmas practices were most significant for me and might delight our children created space to try new things and to graciously release activities that weren't a good fit for our season in life.

So for the past few years, just my daughter and I have started making Christmas candy together, and we often try new recipes. We carefully selected a few favorites from family traditions to begin, and we also made space to develop new favorites and traditions. When my mother-in-law passed away, we added Wheatie Balls (page 162) and caramels to our repertoire to connect our Christmas celebrations with that part of our extended family.

Typically, traditions evolve slowly, over the course of many seasons and in response to varied experiences. When I realized that, most simply, traditions are actions that are repeated, I was able to release some of the angst and pressure to do them all (perfectly). And I was able to reconnect with increased joy and delight. This more gracious and flexible perspective allowed me to engage in practices that were nurturing and meaningful for my own soul. Having less—goodies, decorations, gifts, and activities—felt more aligned with our family's way of life. Thoughtfully choosing from the wide variety of traditions and activities that my husband and I had experienced in our lives allowed us to connect with our heritage and develop a family culture of our own.

The hope celebrated in Advent acknowledges the gap between what exists and what we long to be. It is risky to hope, but the posture of hope allows us to live into the possibility of what could be. Each year as we reflect on the gift of hope, we have the opportunity to begin new traditions and to make new memories.

Intentionally Hopeful Tasks

GWEN

My husband and I were using an open day on the calendar to run errands around town. The extra time together allowed me to off-load my thoughts about a very frustrating work meeting from earlier in the week. Even with the help of Doug's patient ear and working through the problem together from various angles, I couldn't quiet my mind. Eventually, I realized I needed to get my mind off of the difficult meeting and think about something hopeful. Planning and implementing a simple snack and outdoor movie night with several neighbors was just the ticket. Instead of my mind circling a relational problem hopelessly, it was redirected to happy anticipation of time spent with others outdoors.

There are many influences that can lead us away from a hope-filled mindset, and there are many degrees of hopelessness. Some difficulties stay with us, are complex, and require professional help, while others are more easily resolved. Problems inhabit our lives and often need to be addressed directly—I still had to practically engage the problems identified in my work meeting—but choosing to participate in hopeful thoughts and activities in the meantime gave me a chance to reset and analyze those same problems with renewed acceptance and problem-solving energy.

Consciously choose to complete a hopeful task this week. This may require setting some time aside with intentionality. If your schedule feels too full to entertain adding anything, review the week and see if there is something you are already planning to do that could be done with a purposefully hopeful outlook.

As your time allows, consider doing one of the following:

- Spend time wrapping Christmas presents. While you wrap, embrace the hope you have put in the selection that the receiver will enjoy the gift!

- Make something edible that takes time. For example, a dinner from scratch (see bonus recipe for Slow Cooker Cheddar Broccoli Soup on page 161) or festive yeast bread (see Christmas Sweet Bread [*Stollen*] bonus recipe on page 155). While the dinner simmers or the bread rises, take a few moments to enjoy the smell of your intentional creativity. Acknowledge the hope you feel for good nourishment in the future.

- Plan a future flower bed or garden. Enjoy with anticipation and hope the beauty the new garden will bring in the coming year.

Luke 1:39–45

In those days Mary set out and went with haste to a Judean town in the hill country, where she entered the house of Zechariah and greeted Elizabeth.

When Elizabeth heard Mary's greeting, the child leaped in her womb. And Elizabeth was filled with the Holy Spirit and exclaimed with a loud cry, "Blessed are you among women, and blessed is the fruit of your womb. And why has this happened to me, that the mother of my Lord comes to me? For as soon as I heard the sound of your greeting, the child in my womb leaped for joy. And blessed is she who believed that there would be a fulfillment of what was spoken to her by the Lord."

Hope Is Alive

SHERAH-LEIGH

*"And blessed is she who believed that there would be a fulfillment
of what was spoken to her by the Lord."*
—LUKE 1:45

The many opportunities and extra responsibilities of the holiday season can lead us to feel like the stretch between American Thanksgiving and the turn of the new year is one lengthy, frantic hustle. Whether you feel energized and excited by the many to-dos and special events of the season or burdened and weary by the demands (or somewhere in between), the hope celebrated in Advent is that of promises realized.

While many of us are doing the necessary tasks of this week with much *haste*, the hurry demonstrated by Mary in this scripture passage comes from the hope and signs of a promise realized, an overflow of emotion. Mary's haste is not to make things happen, but to celebrate the signs of God's work in her life. She is rejoicing in a dream realized, a promise fulfilled. She honors and proclaims the miracle-in-progress she is experiencing.

And together Mary and Elizabeth's reunion is one of great joy. Something miraculous and unexpected has happened. Hope is alive. There is more to come!

Prophecy is only good news *to those who are hurting*. Resurrection is only possible *when there has been a death*. Hope is only an act of faith when we are in the pit of despair. There is space for both. The call and challenge of Advent is to live within this tension, to experience the truth of both pain and promise.

This is the welcome and warning of Advent:

> Things will change.
> It is not to be like this.
> It will not always be like this.

God, you keep your promises. May my awareness be drawn to the places of hope, the signs of miracles, and the expressions of joy around me. Amen.

Star Bread

SHERAH-LEIGH

Fancy breakfast—namely, homemade cinnamon rolls—was one of the ways my mom tried to make Sundays special for our family. Growing up in a pastor's family meant that weekends looked very different for us than for most of the other people we knew.

While we always ate breakfast together around the table in the mornings, on Sundays we sang a special prayer song and devoured Mom's cinnamon rolls. Our prayer time required each of us to name something we were grateful for. Often as we shared, our private hopes were revealed in what had delighted us or where a need was met.

In this season full of traditions and unique events, consider what parts of each are most meaningful for you. Where are you experiencing hope in the swirl of activity? What are you looking forward to in the coming days? What practices have you carried on from your family of origin? What things have you intentionally shifted to or away from as a way of creating a tradition of your own? What flavors and baked goods bring to mind positive associations with Advent and Christmas? What special treat could you procure or make this week?

Although I don't make cinnamon rolls weekly for my family, I have enjoyed experimenting with baking different kinds of sweet bread. This beautiful star bread looks complicated, but it is simple to make and has a basic form that can work with a wide variety of flavor combinations—from the traditional cinnamon and brown sugar filling to a luscious chocolate hazelnut spread between the layers.

STAR BREAD

Ingredients *for a cinnamon roll–flavored bread*

1 portion bread dough (approximately 1 pound, or the amount of
   dough for one loaf of bread)

For the dough (see bonus recipe for Basic Sweet Bread Dough on
page 152)*, you can use any bread dough. Brioche or any homemade sweetened dough will make these treats richer, but frozen bread dough from the
grocery store will also work and still yield a delicious treat—particularly if
you eat the star bread warm from the oven.*

2 tablespoons unsalted butter, melted
½ cup packed brown sugar, divided equally into two portions
2 tablespoons cinnamon, divided equally into two portions

Method

Allow your dough to complete a first rise. To do so, lightly cover the dough
in a warm place for about 2 hours (longer if you are working with dough
that has been refrigerated or frozen). When the dough has doubled in size,
it is ready to be shaped.

Divide your dough into three equal portions. Roll each portion into a
circle about 12 to 14 inches in diameter. It will be a thin layer of dough, but
don't stretch it so thinly that it tears.

Place the first disc of dough onto a lightly greased 16-inch round or
13 x 9-inch baking sheet. Spread melted butter evenly over dough. Sprinkle
¼ cup of the brown sugar over the buttered dough. Gently shake 1 tablespoon cinnamon in an even layer atop the brown sugar. (You may replace
the butter, brown sugar, and cinnamon with a ¼ cup of your favorite jam,
jelly, or spread for a different flavor profile.) Gently layer the next disc of

dough on top, repeating the method for the filling. Cover with the final portion of dough.

Place a small juice glass or can in the center of the dough. Moving around the circle, use a sharp knife or kitchen shears to cut sixteen equal slices without going through the middle. Twist each slice twice, left to right, to create a swirl effect for each slice of dough. Pinch the ends of two neighboring twisted portions together, forming a point. Do this with neighboring slices around the circle so that you have eight pairs of connected swirls, thus creating the points of your star. If you find that the points are coming apart, slightly moisten your fingertips with water and then pinch the dough again to help the edges seal together.

Allow the star to rise, uncovered, for about 20 to 30 minutes, until doubled.

Bake in an oven preheated to 350°F for 35 to 40 minutes. The star bread should be golden brown when fully baked; check to make sure the dough is completely cooked through at the center.

Yields 8 to 10 servings

Shared Hope

GWEN

When Elizabeth heard Mary's greeting,
the child leaped in her womb.
—LUKE 1:41

Sometimes when we know someone's whole story it inspires us to offer more grace, and sometimes . . . even more hope. It can take something as simple as recognizing a feeling of "been there, done that" to change our perspective. After experiencing years of sitting with my own children through long church services, trying to help them maintain quiet and respectful behavior, I have lots of grace and hope for other families trying to manage these same responsibilities of parenthood. I know that their children, too, will grow up, and what seems overwhelming in the present moment will fade into memory. Nostalgia often fills me now as I watch young children squirm in church.

Other times, knowing someone's heartache through shared stories enables our own gracious and hopeful response. It isn't easy to help shoulder another person's sorrow, but hope is born for both the person receiving care and the caregiver through these interactions.

For me, it isn't hard to imagine why Mary set off to visit her cousin Elizabeth. Elizabeth was older than Mary. Although we don't know for certain by how many years, we know Mary was young and Elizabeth was older than what was considered to be childbearing age. Mary must have heard through the pre–social media grapevine that her cousin Elizabeth was also expecting a miracle child. Elizabeth, who had been barren, and Mary, a virgin, were both pregnant at the same time! What a wonderful opportunity to share in the hope they had received and in the struggle of their mutual situations.

This story is replete with hope, not the least of which is the shared understanding between these two women. They greet one another with joy! Mary and Elizabeth's pregnancies are the fulfillment of prophecies long proclaimed. Even the baby in Elizabeth's womb leaps in the presence of the coming Messiah, not only in acknowledgment of Jesus, but more immediately in response to Mary, a young woman willing to embrace God's work in her life and the role she will play to bring about God's plan for the world.

I have often wondered how much rejection Mary felt during this uncertain time in her life and by contrast, how much support. Just as I have found my own circle of encouraging women, certainly Mary had other Elizabeths in her life—women of faith who had eyes to see the bigger picture and who were able to speak hope-filled words to Mary.

May we, like Elizabeth and Mary, share hope with one another this season.

God, open our eyes so that we can be like Mary and Elizabeth, catching glimpses of your hope-filled bigger picture. Amen.

Unresolved Hope

GWEN

Hope is an unresolved feeling. It is like that microsecond at the top of the roller coaster just before the descent, an almost-moment, which can make us feel a little squirmy. Hope can also be a little scary because it doesn't always work itself out into joy. Sometimes hope is followed by disappointment. The very need for hope implies a person's discontent and longing for change. And change can be difficult, even when it is desired.

After the birth of each of my children, my life was changed. Each child was hoped for and anticipated with equal measures of impatience and joy. I remember sitting on my bed several weeks after the birth of my oldest son, wishing desperately for sleep while trying to work out an insurance coverage gap over the phone as my baby slept. The utter exhaustion and complex issues with our insurance company were not what I had hoped for, but they were part of the journey anyway. The changes brought about by adding an infant to our family were wonderful and overwhelming; something I had fervently hoped for also required adjustment at the same time.

Take some time to write in your journal, talk with a friend, or think about the following reflection questions:

- Name some things you have hoped for and received. Did the results turn out how you expected?

- What are some things you hoped for that never happened? Did the hope become something else? Is it a hope you still have or a longing that was resolved in another way?

- What benefits do you and others receive from being hopeful?

- What dreams or ideas can you hopefully place before God in Advent?

59

Take some deep breaths. Sit quietly. When you are ready, read the prayer of hope below.

God of prophecy, God of the future, pour hope over us this Advent season. May we have the ridiculous courage to be a hopeful people. Not naive or pie-in-the-sky hopeful. Instead, may we be a people who know that you are a faithful God who keeps your promises. With this knowledge and hope-filled hearts, we place our uncertain futures and our sometimes chaotic present into your faithful care. As we plan and experience our holiday moments, may they be infused with your hope and your realized promises. Amen.

Reverence for the Future

GWEN

I grew up in a small, rural valley nestled within the larger Blue Ridge Mountains of Virginia. Each year we cut our Christmas tree from a neighboring field of cedars. Virginia cedars grew like weeds in the pastures and could be rather scraggly looking, but they definitely brought the scent of the season inside. The aroma of fresh, pungent pine filled the house every year. Once we added lights, tinsel, and various ornaments, who minded the less-than-perfect shape? Certainly not my childhood self. When the tree was in place in the family room, there was the hope of gifts to come. And after the gifts were in place, there was the hope of a wonderful surprise when they were opened on Christmas morning.

I remember feeling a bit of scorn—and also shock—upon learning that other families didn't wait until Christmas morning to open presents, opening gifts on Christmas Eve instead. (Picture here a small, wide-eyed child with her hand over her gasping mouth.) Delayed gratification and hopeful waiting were practically a competitive sport in my family. As we waited for gift-opening to commence, we played the game of calculating what was in the packages by shaking and lifting each gift. My brother got so good at guessing that my mom resorted to diversionary tactics, such as adding puzzle pieces and bricks to gift boxes, to throw us all off. She eventually devised a strategy to leave off the name tags altogether. Of course, this plan was risky, as then she needed to remember whose gift was whose on Christmas morning. All this heightened intrigue only increased our delight; brightly wrapped presents lovingly placed beneath the tree were symbols of anticipation and hope.

Hope belongs in the Advent season. The word *advent* means the arrival of some person, thing, or event. And the season of Advent also implies waiting for that special something or someone to arrive. Hope is an essential part of celebrating and understanding Advent. As a child I entered into the hopefulness of the season surrounded by twinkly lights, homemade cookies, and shiny presents under a cedar Christmas tree. Anything might be in those packages. As an adult my hopes still include happy celebrations and presents, but they also extend into the future. I hope for God's presence in my life and in the lives of others, especially the ones I love.

In the meantime, then and now, there was and is a lot of waiting.

It's my own spiritual discipline to recognize God at work, not just as I reflect over the past events of my life, but in the present moment. Often when we look back, we can see all the things that God has done in our own lives or in the lives of others. For me this inspires a feeling of deep reverence. It moves me to realize how God has indeed been with me or with a friend, even when I couldn't recognize it in the moment. For some reason God's presence seems to be more easily identified as we glance back into the past.

Perhaps hope is the inverse of that. Hope allows us to hold this same feeling of reverence we experience when looking back over our life, but instead recognizing it as we look ahead toward events in the future that haven't yet been realized. Hope is believing that God will work in the future like God has in the past. As the author of Hebrews 11:1 writes, "Now faith is the assurance of things hoped for, the conviction of things not seen." I want to have hope that what is happening now will work out for good. This is intrinsically connected to that first type of reverence: because I can see what God has done in the past, I can have confidence for the future.

Biblical stories are full of hopefulness, retelling God's faithful advent into each person's present moment. These stories show that God desires to transform what appears to be hopeless. Hagar ran out into the desert hopeless and alone but met God there. When she left, she could confidently call God "the God who sees me" (Genesis 16:13 NIV). Joseph was sold into slavery by his brothers only to become a powerful advisor to Pharoah. Ruth, a stranger in the land of Israel, became a grandmother in the lineage of Christ. Mary, a young pregnant teenager, became the mother of Jesus. God's provision and hope transformed each person in what were hopeless situations by any human measure.

We look back and draw strength from the historical recounting in the Bible, similar stories in our own lives, and the testimony of other believers. These stories all point to God's faithfulness and become the fuel for the hope we hold out for God's future work in our world.

In the meantime, we wait with expectation in the present moment. What people or dreams do you hold with hope this Advent season? We are fully alert, waiting for God to show up. So clean your metaphorical glasses, remove the spiritual wax from your ears, allow the cedar-pine scent to clear your mind. Look, listen, and wait—hopefully!

Christ was here on earth. We remember and we retell the story.

God is here now. We look for the signs of God's transformative work in our lives.

Jesus is coming again. We hold hope courageously for the future.

Blessing for the Season

SHERAH-LEIGH

May you honor
the unexpected gifts of delight,
even as you go with great haste.

May you savor
the joy and goodness of the now,
trusting as Mary: Blessed!

May all that you bring from seasons past
enliven this one,
exclaiming as Elizabeth: Blessed!

And may all that you choose to carry on
sustain you,
even as you wonder: How can this be?

No matter what unfolds,
may you hold onto hope
for the fulfillment of what the Lord has spoken.
Amen.

WEEK 3

Joy

Blessing for the New Day

SHERAH-LEIGH

Breathe deeply of
the precipitous air

Unfurl your shoulders
turn your face toward the rising sun

Allow the crisp morning air
to fill your lungs

Savor the quiet
moment

Gather what you need to
face the new day

Joy's Interruptive Invitation

GWEN

Just now I was gazing out my front window. It looks out over our porch and to the beds of lavender, where bumble bees are currently buzzing happily among the blossoms. Further out, the four rails of the board fence neatly follow the gentle contour of the newly green lawn. We have been through a very dry spring, and several chilly, wet storm systems have recently restored the lawn and pastures around our house. But this beautiful, ordered view is interrupted by my son's haphazardly parked scooter on the porch. As I take in the full scene, I realize that this everyday picture of beauty and the natural world juxtaposed with my child's carelessly parked toy is the essence of joy. For me, joy is peace interrupted by love.

I know that fierce joy can carry us through painful times as well. When my oldest son was graduating from high school, I felt both joy and sorrow tugging at my mothering heart. Sometimes I felt overwhelmed with sadness that he would be leaving our family home to start his own adult journey, but at the same time such pride and delight in his many accomplishments and success in life so far. My happiness also included excitement as I watched him prepare for the new adventures college would bring. Joy, both in who my son was and could be, was a healing balm during this time of transition.

Over the years of our friendship, Sherah-Leigh and I have savored many conversations together about our families and about life in general. We have spent time reflecting on books and reading. Somewhere along the way, we learned of each other's mutual interest in writing and have encouraged one another in what could otherwise have been a solitary endeavor. We have discussed ideas and explored new ways to think about the world around us. This joint intellectual exercise and pressing onward in creativity has brought much joy into my life.

In the biblical accounts of Jesus' conception and birth, people are surprised by joy. Last week's scripture recounted the story of Elizabeth and Mary's joyful encounter while they were both still expecting. John the Baptist, still a baby in Elizabeth's womb, kicks for joy at Mary's arrival. I wonder what Elizabeth was working on when Mary arrived. Women in the first century had a wide variety of chores to complete to feed and clothe their families. Yet Elizabeth made time and space to be interrupted by Mary's joyful visit.

The shepherds were caring for their sheep in Luke 2. It might not get much more humdrum than that, but then a host of angels appear singing in the night sky. The angels share their message of joy and delight with the shepherds—their Savior has arrived. What a picture of joy interrupting the ordinary!

In Luke 2 we also hear of Anna's joy at seeing the Messiah in her lifetime. Luke tells us that Anna spent decades of her days on earth in the temple praying. Here, in the midst of her daily routine, she is filled with joy and thanksgiving when she sees Jesus with his parents.

These stories remind us that joy often interrupts our everyday lives. Whether you experience joy suddenly or as a slow revelation, I hope you grasp its spiritual significance. Joy contains deep restorative power.

Opening our hearts to experiences of joy and inviting joy into our lives help us to remain resilient. In her book *The Power of Fun*, journalist and screen/life balance expert Catherine Price points out the healing properties of fun.[3] She explains how play, community, and flow can work together to bring restoration into our lives. Having fun and experiencing joy becomes a twofold gift: the feelings of delight give us present happiness and also help to bring about long-term wholeness.

While I know we cannot always grab onto life and demand joy, we can remain expectant. We can be ready to receive joy when God places it in our lives. We can cultivate a life that welcomes laughter and play. In this way, joy offers us another invitation this Advent season.

Welcoming Joy

GWEN

Children bring a special wonder and delight to Christmas endeavors, especially to creative projects. There's plenty we can learn from their carefree, experiential attitudes. When little ones are left to create on their own, they are often unconcerned with the final product. Think of children's instinctive interactions with finger paint, glitter, glue, sprinkles, and frosting! While teachers and parents are busy reminding children to use only what they need, little ones are watching glue pool across their construction paper with joy. Adults just don't get it!

When my now-grown son was a preschooler, I dreaded going into any store with TVs, computers, or any appliance with buttons. He wanted to touch every button. "Mom," he explained, "You don't understand. That's what buttons are for—pushing!" He experienced joy by pushing all the buttons regardless of the outcome. For him, joy was about the process.

Acknowledging that joy has restorative work in our lives look for ways to foster this in yourself and others. Part of welcoming joy into our lives involves releasing control and worry about others' perceptions of us. Children do this so well because they haven't yet learned all of the social rules and constraints that inhibit us adults. Remaining open to joyful surprise is a worthwhile spiritual discipline, no matter what your holiday surroundings might be.

Joy-filled ideas to try:

- Deep breathing can help to solidify a happy memory. This week when you experience something joyful—it can be as small as the smell of holiday cookies baking or a beautiful sunset—pause for a moment to take in what feels joyful. Breathe deeply in and out several times. Imagine adding this moment to your long-term memory. Breathe deeply a few more times.

- Another great way to experience joy is to sing and dance. Instead of having Christmas music on mindlessly in the background this week, pick a few of your favorite songs, crank the volume, sing at the top of your lungs, and dance along!

- Plan a low-stress Christmas party (low stress looks different depending on who you are). Take some time to think of ways to remove stress from hosting your gathering. Keep the food simple: Hello, grocery store freezer department! How about a potluck? Or, just serve one or two special drinks without snacks. Mulled Cider (see bonus recipe on page 160) is just the ticket this time of year.

- Decorate some part of your house without fear of judgment or concern for how others might experience it. Take pleasure in the process instead of being concerned with the outcome.

Luke 1:46–55

And Mary said,
"My soul magnifies the Lord,
   and my spirit rejoices in God my Savior,
for he has looked with favor on the lowly state of his servant.
   Surely from now on all generations will call me blessed,
for the Mighty One has done great things for me,
   and holy is his name;
indeed, his mercy is for those who fear him
   from generation to generation.
He has shown strength with his arm;
   he has scattered the proud in the imagination of their hearts.
He has brought down the powerful from their thrones
   and lifted up the lowly,
he has filled the hungry with good things
   and sent the rich away empty.
He has come to the aid of his child Israel,
   in remembrance of his mercy,
according to the promise he made to our ancestors,
   to Abraham and to his descendants forever."

Joining with God

SHERAH-LEIGH

*And Mary said, "My soul magnifies the Lord, and my spirit
rejoices in God my Savior."*
—LUKE 1:46–47

Being chosen by God for something is wonderful, and Mary responds to God's invitation with joy and hope, reciting the long-awaited promises she has known from her faith tradition. And yet, being chosen by God must also be scary, as the biblical stories of the nativity feature the cry of "Fear not!" after each angelic appearance.

When God's call is revealed in our lives, most often we feel overwhelmed because God asks of us things we cannot do on our own. God invites us to be challenged, to be vulnerable, and to be reliant on the Spirit's guidance.

Our culture argues that pain and discomfort are to be avoided at all costs. But the stories of our faith remind us that grief and joy, lament and rejoicing, and excitement and terror are all a part of what it means to be a disciple of Christ. When God invites us to participate in the kingdom, it requires giving our very selves.

While we may prefer the images of a silent night and the glory of angels appearing, the nativity story reminds us that there is space for any and all of the responses that may be stirred. Hope and promise, yes! But also fear, grief, and loss. Connection and redemption, yes! But also misunderstanding, conflict, and anger.

Perhaps because of its familiarity, we can miss how Mary's song is a beautiful proclamation of God's favor and blessing in the midst of her initial fear and hesitation. Mary yields to God's invitation for her life. What is often reduced to a simple plot point on the timeline of Christ's arrival is a very complex and amazing story of its own. Mary's joy was first an individual and internal faith experience. A series of events with worldwide impact began because of God's specific call to one person who said yes.

And yet to be made fully known to all people, this experience had to unfold over time. Mary's great outpouring of joy required great trust and great patience. The joy expressed here was not simply an emotional response, but also a proclamation of promise. And Mary's joy became an ongoing practice made accessible by connecting with the bigger picture of God's continuing and redeeming work in the world.

These patterns and markers are truths we can see revealed in our own faith journeys. The call and opportunities God gives to each of us can feel overwhelming, even daunting. Often we are asked to step out in faith, extending beyond our abilities or confidence, trusting in the Spirit to guide and inspire our connections and work. And the good gifts of God, while enriching and blessing our own lives, are never just for us. The fruits of our endeavors are for the good of those within our communities. The impact of the good news transforms not just individuals but friends, neighbors, and even enemies.

While God's call and cost may be deeply personal, God's kingdom comes in ways that bring healing, hope, joy, and shalom widely.

God, help me be open to the invitation you have for me. May I experience great joy in partnering with your work in the world. Amen.

Family Fruitcake

SHERAH-LEIGH

For many of us, one of the delights of the holiday season is the special music. While the secular Christmas tunes played on repeat starting as early as Halloween may become tiresome, the sacred refrains of Advent hymns and the familiar lyrics of Christmas carols can stir our hearts in a particular way, often bringing pleasure or a wave of nostalgia.

Music connects to a deeper part of ourselves. Hearing familiar tunes and words memorized long ago can cause a well of emotion in us with just a few notes. Not only do we find comfort in memorized truths that we hold deep in our hearts, we also experience the transcendence of peace and joy in the melodies of music in worship.

We usually think of scripture as text, yet the proclamation attributed to Mary is often referred to as her *song*. The prophet Zechariah also has a poetic recording within the nativity narrative in Luke 1:67–79, but it is the familiar words of Mary's song recorded in the gospel of Luke that speak not only to her personal present experience, but connect her and her community to the rich tradition of faithfulness and provision while proclaiming the hope and vision for justice in God's coming reign.

Just like the strains of music, flavors and spices can also call forth memories, connecting us with our families and traditions. They tap into another sense that when stimulated draws us deeper into the holiday experience. Our minds may connect with musical tunes when our other faculties fail us, and our sense of smell has a significant role in conjuring memories and pleasure.

A few years ago, my father reminisced about the fruitcake his mother made for the Christmases he experienced as a boy. At first, I turned my nose up at the idea of making a fruitcake (all the cultural jokes about it being inedible and such); this was not a treat that had made it into our contemporary family tradition. But as the days drew me toward our Christmas meal, I thought it would be a special gift to surprise my dad with a taste from his childhood.

While my first few attempts didn't quite hit the mark, the look of joy on my father's face when he tried the final version was worth all the effort. This recipe is now emerging as a newly beloved tradition for our family. I have made it yearly for the past few years, and it is a recipe I will pass on to future generations, since despite the many Christmas treats available, there is rarely any fruitcake left on the serving platter!

FAMILY FRUITCAKE

Ingredients
2 cups pitted dates
1¼ cups candied pineapple
1¼ cups candied cherries
½ cup candied orange peel
2 cups all-purpose flour
2 teaspoons baking powder
¼ teaspoon salt
2 eggs
½ cup granulated sugar
1 teaspoon almond extract
3¾ cups chopped walnuts (or any combination of your favorite nuts)
2 tablespoons corn syrup

Method
First, coarsely chop the dates and candied fruits and set aside. In a large bowl, mix together the flour, baking powder, and salt. Add the chopped dates and candied fruits to the bowl. Toss the flour mixture with the chopped fruit until the pieces are evenly coated.

In a small bowl, beat the eggs, sugar, and almond extract. When the eggs are frothy, pour this mixture over the prepared fruit. Gently fold in the nuts, combining carefully until the batter completely coats the nuts and fruit. The filling should be lightly covered with batter and not clumped.

Transfer the mixture into a greased 9-inch springform pan, packing it in firmly to hold together. This batter should fill the pan to the edges and top.

Bake in a preheated oven at 275°F for 90 minutes, or until the batter is cooked through. When baked, the edges will be lightly browned and the top will no longer be gooey or sticky to the touch.

Allow to stand for 5 to 10 minutes on a cooling rack before releasing the sides of the pan.

While still warm, brush fruitcake with the corn syrup to add a nice shine.

Cool completely and slice to enjoy. This fruitcake can be made ahead and stored in the fridge or freezer for up to two months.

Yields 1 cake (24 servings)

Joy beyond Our Circumstances

GWEN

> *"He has brought down the powerful from their thrones*
> *and lifted up the lowly;*
> *he has filled the hungry with good things*
> *and sent the rich away empty."*
> **—LUKE 1:52–53**

O ver and over in the Bible this message is repeated: our circumstances are not what bring us joy. This concept is a hard sell in our modern culture of convenience and wealth. We are told daily—as we interact with others on social media, hear commercials, shop in stores, or take in the news—that what we currently have is not enough. The push is so strong to acquire more that we must have an active mindset in the opposite direction to resist the pressure. It is easy to believe that if I just had a little more of some elusive thing, I would feel joyful, content, or at peace.

In Mary's Magnificat (Luke 1:46–55), she points out the upside-down kingdom coming to pass, where God's son is born not to Herod or into anyone else's powerful, wealthy family, but to a young woman living in Galilee. Everything appears wrong-footed, but at the same time exactly what God had planned. I wonder what the Pharisees would have had to say about the woman God had chosen to birth and raise the Messiah if they had known of his arrival in advance. They probably would have questioned God's plan. Throughout the New Testament, despite their apparent status and wealth, the Pharisees do not come across as a joyful group of people.

In contrast, Mary jubilantly sings, "He has brought down the powerful from their thrones and lifted up the lowly" (Luke 1:52). Years later, Jesus taught, "And why are you anxious about clothing? Consider the lilies of the field, how they grow, they neither toil nor spin, yet I tell you, even Solomon in all his glory was not arrayed like one of these" (Matthew 6:28–29). Jesus did not share this counsel with a group of people who had closets full of clothing or access to our modern conveniences. Comparatively, Jesus' audience had much less financial security than many of us do today, yet Jesus exhorted them not to worry.

Despite all that we own, we are very anxious people. According to the World Health Organization, depression and anxiety are some of the most common health concerns worldwide.[4] Clearly, anxiety isn't resolved by consumerism.

Whether anxiety is a fleeting challenge or a daily struggle for you, the Advent season is rife with opportunities to experience joy. For me, it is the moment the door opens and I welcome my family and friends for a celebration, or taking time to soak in the beauty of decorated houses throughout the neighborhood. Sometimes joy is hearing beautiful music in the company of others at a Christmas concert. Joy can be found examining the biblical Christmas story with new eyes, looking for and contemplating the upside-down, joy-filled kingdom of God. I hope you can embrace whatever nurtures joy in your heart and allows you to set aside your anxious thoughts this Advent season.

God who knows my anxious thoughts, I welcome you into my heart in preparation for the upcoming Christmas season. Give me courage to trust you and embrace joy in the beautiful moments that you send my way this Advent. Amen.

Deep Joy

GWEN

If happiness is generated by external circumstances, then joy must come from a deeper place. Mary sings for joy even though there is also disappointment and hardship in the invitation and miracle God has given her. She has a bigger picture of God's plan beyond herself, which in turn increases her joy. Like Mary, we can choose to participate in the world around us and take part in God's purpose even when we experience difficulty.

Engaging joy despite our circumstances can take many forms. Mary said yes to becoming the mother of the Son of God and expressed her joy in song. The gift of her creative response lives on for us to enjoy many years later. Our vocations and church communities are two among many places to gain perspective and joy in service to others. By connecting to experiences beyond ourselves, whether a mission or a community group, we can gain a new perspective and encouragement.

Learning to recognize and experience joy despite our circumstances involves welcoming light and wonder into our lives in little ways too. Sometimes a bad day is also sprinkled with small but meaningful moments of delight. A delicate flower, a smiling child, and a deep, full breath of air, can all trigger a feeling of contentment and gladness. Acknowledging that each day and stage of life has both hardship and goodness can open our spirits, allowing joy to blossom despite difficult situations.

Spend some time considering these questions. Feel free to reflect in your journal or share some of your responses with trusted friends.

- What has God invited you to do?

- When have you said yes to God and experienced great joy?

- What dream do you have for your life that intersects with God's calling?

- What part of that vision can you rejoice in today?

- What are some small moments of joy you have experienced today?

God of creativity, laughter, and joy, we welcome you! Open our eyes to see and experience joy when it arrives. Give us gracious, flexible hearts. We want to celebrate the light of this season and the gift of your Son. We confess that in our efforts to control the outcome, we can miss the joy of the moment. May we be not only receivers of joy but co-creators with you, God of gladness and restoration. Amen.

Greater Joy

SHERAH-LEIGH

*G*wen and I became friends a bit before we considered ourselves to be in midlife, and we have certainly waded our way through bouts of significant stress and unhappiness together over the years. We have discerned job changes, tackled career questions, released some visions for our lives, and imagined new possibilities. We have celebrated wins and successes and wept on each other's shoulders. We have packed (and unpacked) boxes, shifted furniture, wiped down shelves and traded childcare when we have moved houses. And perhaps most notably, we have both navigated the health declines and terminal diagnoses that have led to the loss of a parent-in-law. In some stretches of life, joy has merely seemed a mirage.

But apparently (and perhaps counterintuitively), research suggests women's happiness increases as they get older. American psychologist and author Mary Pipher writes and reflects on the experience of aging, noting that our happiness is correlated with our ability to hold appropriate expectations and to be adaptable.[5]

A cursory online search of the differences between joy and happiness yields an interesting result. *Fleeting, circumstantial, emotional,* and *self-focused* were all attributes of happiness, which contrasts with the understanding that joy is a gift from God and an inner sense of being. But no matter how you define it, by this point in the Advent season, being holly-jolly and merry and bright is often rather difficult, especially as the number of events ramp up and the hours to wrap up the holiday to-do list diminish all too quickly. And that doesn't account for how an ill-timed stomach bug or snowstorm may upend anticipated gatherings or travel plans.

The problem with joy is that when it is prescribed or desired, it is least likely to manifest. There's a cultural assumption that this is the most wonderful time of the year. And when our feelings don't fall in line, the pressures of how we (think we) *should* be in the experience only add to the disappointments and gloom.

For many, this season is the worst time of year. When the stretches of light are limited, and the weather in many places curtails outdoor activities and routines, the long dark days of winter are bleak. Add in the memories of family traditions past that can no longer be recreated or the realities of the ever-changing configurations of life that might limit the making of holiday memories we had hoped for, nostalgia and pain from our family legacies can bring anguish.

In the midst of grief, holiday cheer can be particularly challenging to connect with as you navigate the firsts without a loved one and face the reality that some things are forever changed.

Yet somehow, miraculously and beautifully, in the face of loss there can also be moments of greater joy. The intensity of emotion magnified by grief isn't just around sadness; delight and pleasure can also be increased. The limitations and bounds of time are part of what brings meaning to our lives. Time is neither guaranteed nor constant, and that preciousness infuses joy into our sacred and ordinary. Being reminded of this reality can renew our appreciation for some things and allow us to extend more grace in others. The clarity that comes with grief helps us prioritize which legacies and traditions we want to shape in our own families.

In light of the interplay between grief and goodness in your own life, how might you assume a posture primed for joy? How can you remain open with hope to the possibility of being surprised by the miraculous, the unexpected turning? How can you hold on to the experience of God with us?

Whether joy is a gift you are unwrapping this week or a distant memory of a past season of life, may you recalibrate your expectations and remain flexible, embracing the good in the present moment with thanksgiving.

Christmas Prayer

GWEN

Holy God,

With Mary
we are people of our time and place,
wondering at the miracle of your Son.
Our hearts sing praise
while our minds struggle to accept the mystery.
Our arms are reaching;
we welcome the unexpected gifts of this season.

Thank you.
Again,
you arrive in our homes and
our hearts.

We welcome you in, Lord Jesus.
Rearrange our worn-out expectations.
Give us
eyes to see your beauty,
ears to hear your call,
hands and feet to enact your love in the world.

May we, like Mary,
accept with humility and joy
your gift,
embracing the
warmth and surprise of the
newborn Son of God.
Amen.

WEEK 4

Peace

Holiday Communing

GWEN

Wish lists exchanged
Litanies of
Mermaids
Dump trucks
Dinosaurs
Gift cards purchased

Recipes bookmarked
Cookies baked
Worry and anticipation mingle

Guest rooms dusted and polished
Meals planned
Phone calls and texts
Electronic prayers
Wing across the miles
What will you bring?
When will you arrive?

Mantel decorated
Special napkins washed
Presents wrapped and waiting

"What's your ETA?"

They arrive from distant planets
Brooklyn and Illinois
With bags and good cheer
Hugs surround us all as the
cold air blows
them in the door

Fussy and excited children
Beeline for the toy closet
The house is bursting
My heart as well

Naps negotiated
Presents opened
Bread is broken
Meals consumed
Cookies praised

Days
navigating each person's space
Who eats what?
When and where?
Some sleep, others don't
Quiet?
Loud?

Introverts and extroverts
bump around the house
Oops! Don't talk about that!
How do we have the same parents?

But then
Connections thrown across the living room
and caught
The hours fly
in the hymn of family conversation

Abruptly,
Before we're ready
Cousins yell goodbye
Cars are packed
Hugs again
Wheels turn
Doors close

Dust settles like a blessing on the living room
All is quiet
Sadness mixes quietly with relief
The house is empty
My heart is full of
Holiday stillness.

All Is Well

SHERAH-LEIGH

A favorite Christmas song in our household is "All Is Well," a beautiful proclamation of the promise of Advent realized. It is a moving piece written by Michael W. Smith, and it always stirs something deep in me, whether I'm listening to the piano-led version or to a live performance with a full choir. There is something truly peaceful about the vision and hope celebrated by this song.

With so much unsettled in the world around us, at times it is challenging to hold the paradox of the song, which names the already and not yet nature of God's kingdom. At Christmas we celebrate the incarnation and the good gifts that come with Jesus' arrival. And yet, we live in a time and place where we are still impacted by conflicts, sickness, and sin.

While *peace* can evoke a number of things, in the Advent season the word appears in carols and Christmas wishes as a longed-for state of being. It may stand in stark contrast to our experience of the hustle and bustle of activities and demands that the countdown to Christmas brings. Peace may feel like a pipe dream in the face of contentious family relationships, strained budgets, and unending expectations. But peace in this context is a state of being, despite the circumstances. It is a certain groundedness and inner resolve that allows one to engage the relationships, tasks, and challenges of each day in a particular way: accessing hope, responding graciously, being generous with love, and living free from anxiety.

So how do we receive this gift of peace? How do we connect with the *all is well* sentiment when balls are dropping, Murphy's Law takes full effect, or there simply aren't enough hours in the day?

The invitation to experience peace is always before us; when we engage in the practices that ground us in God's faithfulness, take notice of the natural rhythm of all things, and remember proportion and perspective, we can again settle ourselves in the peace that Jesus gives.

Creation surrounds us and can be grounding and renewing, whether we are delighting in the comforts of the familiar views from our front porches or the backyard of our childhood home, or experiencing the wonder of exploring a different landscape in a place we have never been before. Our awe and connection to God can be stoked by the beauty, intricacy, and scale of nature.

The second-story deck at Gwen's home offers a panoramic view of the indigo and gray Blue Ridge Mountain range. We have sipped tea together in her soft swivel chairs while having our monthly book club discussion. We have sliced layered cake, gathering around the long-planked table to celebrate birthdays with loved ones. We have drafted reflections, sitting side by side with our old laptops, which are plugged into extension cords poking out through the screen door. Whether in our chatter over rom-com tropes, shared laughter over kids' knock-knock jokes, or in the whispered conversations that bear witness to our deepest sorrows, the beauty of the mountain peaks and rolling fields has been the setting and anchor for many sacred moments.

With or without a mountain view, we have access to these holy spaces—places that connect us with the goodness and grandeur of God's creation. And when we take time to enter into them and take a moment to exhale, we experience a renewed sense of peace.

I have resided in two different countries and three different states (so far!), yet I have always experienced all four seasons. Of course, I have my favorite, but there is beauty to be found in each, whether taken in from Gwen's back deck in Virginia or the glider on my front porch in Ohio. The bright greening of spring, the long-light days of peak summer, the vibrant coloring of autumn leaves, or the glistening stillness of a blanket of snow—all fill me with a sense of peace.

Where do you experience a physical grounding in the peace of Christ? What view or connection with creation can you take in today that will renew and calm you? How might elements of the natural world connect you with a deeper inner peace?

While the many demands of this season paired with the challenges of daily life may not be easily relieved or resolved, accessing the peace that transcends understanding and circumstance may be surprisingly easy. A breath of fresh air, inhaling the scent of spruce and pine boughs, and a moment of pause gazing upon a serene landscape are all opportunities to find ourselves within the bigger picture of God's good creation. And they allow our attention to be refocused into the sacred ordinary available to us in the present moment.

Breathing Deeply

GWEN

Breathing deeply is perhaps one of the simplest and most profound ways to bring the body, mind, and spirit into one peaceful spot. When I swim laps, I am forced to breathe at specific times during my stroke. This repetitive action expands my lungs and relaxes my body. When I feel anxious, few actions are as calming as deep breaths. Isn't it interesting that during the labor of childbirth, a time of deep creativity and pain, one of the tried-and-true techniques for the journey is focused breathing?

Take time to try out some of these breathing techniques this week as a way of bringing peace to your soul.

- Breath prayers are short prayers that can be repeated throughout the day, as you intentionally breathe in and out. Some examples to try include:

    Emmanuel (*inhale*), God with us (*exhale*)

    Peace (*inhale*), be still (*exhale*)

- Many types of physical exercise help you to focus on breathing and allow you to come away refreshed having engaged in healthy self-care and hopefully feeling more at peace in your body. Yoga, swimming, and weightlifting are a few examples of activities that encourage breathing at specific times during intentional movement. Consider focusing on your breath as you exercise this week or add a new exercise that helps you feel at peace.

- Box breathing is a visualization technique designed to help you slow down your breathing and relax. Imagine drawing one side of a rectangle at a time in your mind as you complete the steps for breathing. You can draw the box in the air together using your fingers while you slow your breathing. (This practice also works well with children.)

Breathe in deeply for about 3 seconds (*draw first side of the box*).

Hold your breath for about 3 seconds (*draw second side of the box*).

Exhale slowly for about 3 seconds (*draw third side of the box*).

Hold your breath for about 3 seconds (*draw fourth side of the box*).

Repeat as needed.

Matthew 1:18–25

Now the birth of Jesus the Messiah took place in this way.

When his mother Mary had been engaged to Joseph, but before they lived together, she was found to be pregnant from the Holy Spirit. Her husband Joseph, being a righteous man and unwilling to expose her to public disgrace, planned to divorce her quietly.

But just when he had resolved to do this, an angel of the Lord appeared to him in a dream and said, "Joseph, son of David, do not be afraid to take Mary as your wife, for the child conceived in her is from the Holy Spirit. She will bear a son, and you are to name him Jesus, for he will save his people from their sins."

All this took place to fulfill what had been spoken by the Lord through the prophet:

> "Look, the virgin shall become pregnant and give birth to a son,
> and they shall name him Emmanuel,"

which means, "God is with us." When Joseph awoke from sleep, he did as the angel of the Lord commanded him; he took her as his wife but had no marital relations with her until she had given birth to a son, and he named him Jesus.

Choose Wisely

SHERAH-LEIGH

But just when he had resolved to do this, an angel of the Lord appeared to him in a dream and said, "Joseph, son of David, do not be afraid . . ."
—MATTHEW 1:20

I felt weary from the many forms of labor associated with moving and overwhelmed by the prospect of networking and processing job options in my new town. "I'm just trying to thread the needle between patient trust and proactive connection," I lamented to my friend over our daily video message. While the concept of discernment may sound spiritually grounded and gentle, anyone who has navigated a slow transition knows that the discomfort of the unknown and in between is not for the faint of heart.

Decision fatigue. Analysis paralysis. *Perfect is the enemy of good.* We've all been there. Whether we fear making a mistake, desire to maximize an opportunity, or lack confidence, when it's decision time, we long for clarity. If only God would send an angelic messenger to tell us what to do next!

However, Joseph's angelic message is not one of confirmation but challenge. Are we willing to accept the call and instruction of God when it turns our plans, ideas, or anticipation upside down? In our prayerful discernment, are we open to signs and messages from God no matter the content, or are we only looking for affirmation of the path we have already determined in our hearts?

In discernment and in faith, the context matters. The biblical narrative is rife with examples of when the right response was a yes, and other times assent to God's way meant saying no to others. Sometimes people were called to go somewhere new. Other times the command was to stay. Sometimes the Spirit prompted people to speak; other times, the instruction was to be silent. The common thread throughout the account of God and God's people has been patient listening.

"Often when we are in a period of discernment our hearts become noisy with choices and possibilities. We try to think our way through things to an outcome," writes Christine Valters Paintner in her book, *Birthing the Holy*. She notes that we live in a culture that is resistant to slowing down, of making space. But in our efforts to endlessly produce, we do deep damage to ourselves and others. "As Mary teaches us, creativity isn't always about doing and producing; it is also about incubating and gestating."[6]

We all long to experience peace in our lives, particularly when we make a choice or decision. In picking a path, we hope for the certainty and comfort of the peace that transcends understanding as confirmation. But peace may involve more than a feeling of settledness or resolve that comes from making the right decision. Divine peace may more often arrive surprisingly, without change to our circumstances or situations.

We are invited to birth the holy in our own lives. Might the faithful response to God's invitation be patient waiting? Embracing a threshold? Quiet growth or maturation? Sometimes the gift of peace comes in surprising and unexpected ways. It is not something we can choose or manufacture. In the situations where we are longing and impatient, in circumstances where we are struggling and striving, the weeks of waiting in Advent remind us that peace is a blessing to receive, not a task to accomplish. Sometimes peace arrives suddenly and sometimes incrementally; it is always a gift we receive.

May I trust you, O God, in the threshold spaces of my life. May I have abundant patience as I discern, release, and wait. And may I joyfully receive the gift of true peace that only comes from you. Amen.

Ranch Party Mix

SHERAH-LEIGH

Many families go big when it comes to feasting, but my Mennonite families take it to the extreme! Most of my grandmother Dorothy Risser's diary entries include menus and garden reports. I remember my mother, who trained as a home economics teacher (and then as a pastor), recalling the "seven sweets and seven sours" rule of thumb that dictated the spread of any meal her family hosted for guests on their Lancaster County dairy farm.

My Canadian Mennonite Zehr family also has a wonderful heritage of good food, and they are particularly excellent at producing snacks. Whether meant to supplement the time of conversation and games surrounding Christmas dinner, or to nibble on in the lodge for a few days at the summer family reunion, there is never a shortage of goodies, and each of my dad's siblings has a traditional contribution we all eagerly expect.

My paternal grandmother always made a huge batch of "scrabble" (a particular form of party mix) that tastes the best when made with Trix fruity breakfast cereal. At one point, the batches she made were so large, she mixed them in a (new) trash bag.

While I am more partial to the traditional party mix (which is distinct from scrabble), there is a wide variety of takes on and adaptations of cereal-based snack mixes. At Christmas, there is always a tin of scrabble, another of caramel corn, and one of Ranch Party Mix, which has become our family favorite twist on party mix.

RANCH PARTY MIX

Ingredients
2 (14-ounce) bags crispy corn snacks (such as Bugles)
1 (16-ounce) bag mini twist pretzels
1 (6-ounce) package small cheddar crackers (such as Goldfish)
1 (8-ounce) box miniature buttery crackers (such as Ritz Bitz)
1 (8.5-ounce) box thin wheat baked snack crackers (such as Wheat Thins)
1 (12-ounce) box cheddar snack crackers (such as Cheese Nips)
1 (10-ounce) jar butter-flavored popcorn oil
2 (1-ounce) packets ranch salad dressing seasoning

Method
Gently stir together all of the dry ingredients (crispy corn snacks through cheddar snack crackers). This recipe yields a large amount, so you may need to portion out the crunchy components among a few large bowls or use a large clean tote or washtub to toss the ingredients together. Once all the dry goods are mixed together, set aside.

In a small bowl, whisk together the jar of popcorn oil and ranch salad dressing seasoning until well combined. Pour the flavored oil mixture over your mix of snacks, stirring or shaking gently to coat all the pieces evenly.

Transfer the party mix to several ungreased, rimmed baking sheets and/or roasting pans. Depending on the size of your pans and oven, you may need to bake this in two batches.

Bake at 250°F for 45 minutes, stirring every 15 minutes.

Spread baked mix onto a clean countertop to cool. (I like to cut open some paper grocery bags to line my counter and absorb the extra oils.) The party mix can be stored in an airtight container for up to six weeks.

Yields approximately 30 servings

WEEK 4 ✳ WORDS OF COMFORT

Grace and Peace to You

GWEN

But just when he had resolved to do this, an angel of the Lord
appeared to him in a dream.
—MATTHEW 1:20

I did not grow up in a grace-based religion. It's not that grace wasn't spoken of in my rural Mennonite church—it was! It's just that somewhere along the line I came to understand that, while I was saved by grace, there was a lot of work I needed to do between now and when I reached the pearly gates. This idea was both literal and spiritual.

Many expressions of Anabaptism were formed in farming communities. And if you have lived in a farm family, you know there is usually plenty of work to be done! The work ethic cultivated within my own Mennonite heritage was held with reverential fervor. Mennonites also believe living out a holy life is an important expression of faith. Spirituality isn't limited to attending Sunday service but may affect the type of clothes you wear, the car you drive, and the people you relate to on a daily basis. While I did not grow up on a farm or have to wear a certain type of clothing, I did absorb many of these traditional values applied in new ways to my daily life.

To be clear, I am thankful for the strong work ethic and call to faithful engagement of good works that I inherited from my Mennonite tradition. As in any faith tradition, this emphasis has its pros and cons. Much of my adult life I have spent time struggling with the balance between the assurance of God's saving grace and the call to do faithful, good work in the world. I have held various jobs over the years, striving to balance my work ethic, my pursuit of holy living, and realistic expectations in balance. I have failed much of the time.

I have gradually come to understand the idea that God pursues *us* in love; we do not need to prove ourselves worthy. Even before I complete a single good deed, God loves me. This has brought some peace to my inner struggle between grace and works. Trying to embody my faith out of gratefulness for God's abiding presence and love, rather than out of an obligation to work harder in order to earn God's favor, changes the way I show up in the world. It means I take a deep breath before I say yes to another commitment. I still say yes to many activities and obligations; that's part of life! However, I now know that the many tasks I choose to do each day do not change God's ever-present love for me. At the same time, I have begun to see God's present and future kingdom as an inexorable movement forward, with or without my help. This too has been an immense relief.

In this week's lectionary reading from Matthew 1, an angel appears to Joseph in a dream. Most likely Joseph did not have access to written scriptures. He wasn't part of a culture where the wonders of dreaming were explained through psychology. God used an avenue to communicate that Joseph left open, a dream, to send him a message. This is amazing, since on his own Joseph would have done the kind and culturally appropriate thing of "divorcing Mary quietly" (Matthew 1:19). Instead, God pursued Joseph through a dream to bring about God's loving plan to save God's people. By God's loving grace, Joseph was not left alone to discern the correct path before him.

God still pursues us today. Maybe not with dreams . . . or maybe so. But God's love does search for us and find us, inviting us to participate in bringing God's plan into the world. Our job is to listen with the door of our heart open, be willing to wait, and trust that God will come with grace and be with us. Knowing that God—in an effort to share love with us—seeks us has brought a sense of peace to my spiritual journey. We, like Joseph, are invited to accept God's gracious gift of love and the peace it can bring this Advent season.

God, thank you for seeking and pursuing us with your love. May we accept the grace and peace you extend to each of us. Amen.

One Task at a Time

GWEN

There is no doubt that many people participating in North American culture hold productivity in high esteem. This value does deserve an important place in our lives; hard, effective work can be a balm to our bodies and to our souls. But constantly striving without times of reflection and peace can also lead to a life that feels like running on a hamster wheel.

Special times of focus during the church calendar can provide a path for reevaluation and renewal. Maybe you struggle with the level of busyness or stress in this season, or maybe your enthusiasm for holiday magic is overwhelming your loved ones and friends. Take some time during this week of Advent to consider how you could change your approach to the holiday to-do list you (or maybe those around you) are struggling to complete.

In your journal or on a piece of paper, write out all the things that are waiting to be done (or maybe that you were hoping others would do for you).

It can be helpful to focus on what is next instead of looking at the whole picture all at once. There is always more that could be done. Accepting that we will not be able to do everything can be a step toward fully enjoying the things we can accomplish.

With this thought in mind, and reflecting on the list you created, prioritize what is truly most important for the day ahead.

Take a deep breath and focus on completing those few tasks, taking time to enjoy the process.

God, thank you for the ebb and flow of life. Thank you for busy times with work to complete. Thank you also for times designed to quiet myself before you. (Sit quietly for several minutes, releasing the week ahead to God.) *Thank you for this Advent season and these moments to reflect on your presence with me. Help me to maintain perspective and to receive your steadfast love.* (Breathe deeply for several moments.) *Amen.*

Winter Mornings

GWEN

When I was a school-aged girl, I would lie very still in bed early on winter mornings and listen for traffic on the highway near our house in rural Virginia. I was actually listening for a lack of noise. If there was a muffled silence, with no sounds of traffic, that usually meant one thing—snow! And snow meant sledding, hot chocolate, and maybe even homemade doughnuts were in the near future.

Later, when I graduated from college and went into the teaching profession, I looked forward to snow days for similar reasons. I wasn't alone in wishing for snow days. My teaching colleagues followed many rituals to help ensure snow days when the weather person predicted possible accumulation. Some teachers told their students if they flushed an ice cube down the toilet or wore their pajamas backward it would surely snow that night. Others checked every local weather forecast repeatedly throughout the day: would it snow or not? All this for one, maybe two if we were lucky, unexpected days of peace—a quick hop off the unrelenting treadmill of the school year.

Even now I listen carefully in the early morning hours of winter for the peaceful quiet of snow. Snuggled in bed, I savor that moment of suspense and hush, just hoping. I love the way the snow covers everything, hiding so many imperfections. The traffic slows, and my planned schedule is usually disrupted. Where I live in the Shenandoah Valley, the snow often melts quickly and life returns to normal again. But the shoveling and disturbed schedule are worth the fleeting moments of beauty the snow creates.

Over the years I have heard many sermons and seminars and read literature that dismiss the idea of peace as nothing more than a symptom of a satiated aristocracy. Or sometimes as an overused wish of naive children at Christmastime. I have also seen peace proclaimed publicly while private pain is ignored.

It is true that peace and justice are elusive and sometimes mutually exclusive. However, the Bible speaks of peace as something both God and humanity long to attain. Many passages from the book of Isaiah speak to God's vision for peace for all of God's creation. "The wolf shall live with the lamb; the leopard shall lie down with the kid; the calf and the lion will feed together; and a little child shall lead them," we read in Isaiah 11:6. When Jesus is born in Bethlehem, he fulfills the prophecy of a Messiah who will bring peace and repair the covenant between God and humanity. The angels sing of peace to the shepherds. And in the gospel of Mark, Jesus himself laments, even in the midst of his triumphal ride into the city, "If you, even you, had only recognized on this day the things that make for peace!" (Luke 19:42).

So, it is not a surprise that many modern Christmas songs retell the hope of Emmanuel, God with us, and express a longing for peace. It is not trivial to hope for peace. This desire for peace points us in the direction of God's loving kingdom. Yes, peace involves the hard work of reconciliation within our own inner lives, between us and our neighbors, and more broadly throughout the world. The reality that we have not attained peace does not negate its essential part of our spiritual growth.

Peace straddles the already and not yet nature of Advent. Jesus modeled how to live at peace with our neighbors. He spoke of inner heart work leading to outer fruits of the Spirit. And ultimately he came to earth to renew the covenant of love between God and all people on earth. At Christmas, we celebrate the miracle of Jesus' birth and we live in hope of the peaceful kingdom yet to come.

In what areas of your life are you longing for God's peace? How are you experiencing the already and not yet of Advent?

This year I'm hoping for a little snow if simply to be reminded of God's peace present in Bethlehem long ago, in my home today, and for all of creation in the future.

Blessing for Peace

SHERAH-LEIGH

May you hold your plans and resolves loosely enough
that you can flex with the wind of the Spirit.

And in the midst of invitation and fear,
may you join in being a witness to fulfillment.

In your wondering and waiting,
may there be peace.

In your discerning and deciding,
may there be peace.

In your doing and being,
may there be peace.

WEEK 5

Love

Winter Sunrise

SHERAH-LEIGH

This morning the sun rose,
slowly climbing above the mountain range,
radiating in shades of deep pink and violet.

The bare trees stood black in relief against the vibrant sky.
In minutes it was done,
replaced by pale blue and
the faint cream line above the peaks;
Did I imagine it?

Or perhaps it was a gift—
For the select few awake,
for those who paused to pay attention,
to drink it in like the first warm notes of morning coffee.

The Story of Loving Friendship

GWEN

In the cold winter months of my childhood, the best spot in our house was close to the woodstove. There was a small nook behind the stove that shared a wall with the kitchen; this made the ideal spot to stand and warm up or to perch on the stool that was often tucked into this space. This was also the place where my mother set large bowls of bread dough to rise. At Christmastime this meant *julekake* or *stollen*, a sweet bread with candied fruits and raisins, could be found rising quietly in the warmth (see bonus Christmas Sweet Bread [*Stollen*] recipe on page 155). Its presence signaled to the household a scrumptious breakfast soon, where we could all enjoy slices of sweet bread with butter, and also the commencement of Christmas celebrations.

Looking back, I realize the intricate bread was symbolic of my mother's love and care for her family. This familial love is one of the kinds of love we often celebrate through the traditions we carry out at Christmas.

Sometimes this love between family members and friends is shared through food, and sometimes it is shared in stories we tell as we reminisce during the many social events that punctuate the holidays. Stories encourage us to be our best selves by sharing humor and mutual experiences. You are blessed indeed if you have a gifted storyteller at your holiday gathering. Bible stories are similar in their ability to connect with our emotions and our humanity. The scriptures that retell Jesus' birth are often referred to as "The Christmas Story." This story appears in plays and picture books during the holiday season to help us connect with Jesus' birth so long ago. Stories, whether told by friends and family or read in the Bible, recount God's presence and remind each of us of God's loving work in our lives and in our world.

This is important work. Though we may believe and trust God's love is present, we also know evil is present in this world. Part of what makes relationships with each other so essential is our ability to lift one another up during hard times by reminding each other of God's love and of our love for one another.

A number of years ago, I sought counseling during a particularly difficult time for my family. Multiple factors had brought about an abrupt career change, significant increase in stress, and disconnection from long-term friendships. My counselor was gentle with me, allowing me time to sit and cry quietly, with tears of exhaustion trailing down my cheeks. I learned, and continue to relearn, that sometimes life is just plain difficult. There are no easy answers to many tough questions and situations. One of the most practical bits of counsel she gave me was twofold. Number one, you are not alone. Number two, lest you forget number one, you need to seek out and cultivate meaningful friendships. We all need friends and community. We can experience God's love through the loving care of others in our community.

My counselor was right, of course. She was speaking to me about one of our essential human longings—the desire to be loved. Friendship is a God-given way to communicate and receive love. Jesus had twelve disciples, or close friends, who listened and walked with him during his time here on earth; even God incarnate needed friends. My counselor's advice was vital, and years later it continues to remind me to seek out friends. We cannot happily or fully live life alone. Love needs community and friendship to grow. Reciprocally, we need love to thrive.

Experiencing God's love is a reminder that God did not leave us alone in the world but surrounded us with the opportunities to experience love.

And this is where the Advent journey is bringing us—to love. Just as the people in the biblical Christmas story found support through community and friendship, we approach Christmas Day understanding God's love in part through our experience of love from friends and family. This week we peer into the manger amazed along with Mary, Joseph, and the shepherds, to find the Son of God in our midst. We witness God's love, so full and complete, so unfailing that despite our unfaithfulness, God continues to show up and reach out to the people of the world.

Feel the Love

SHERAH-LEIGH

Sometimes the work of faith is described within the categories of believing, belonging, and behaving. While at various points in history these may have been understood as an expected progression for a person of faith, in our current context, these segments exist in our lives more as a Venn diagram of overlapping circles. Sometimes our behavior leads to our belonging. Other times our places of belonging inform our beliefs. And often what we believe impacts both where we belong and how we behave!

As followers of Jesus, we spend a lot of time and energy focused on emulating Christ. We work to align our practices and behaviors with our beliefs and understanding of scripture. At certain points, we can become very outward-focused in our signs of faith. Other times, we can get caught up in trying to earn our salvation, working hard in acts of service, and forcing transformation of our habits, actions, and words.

Both inner work and outward practices have a significant impact on our spiritual journey. And yet, the foundation of the Christmas message is that God deeply loves us, just as we are. The incarnation, the divine appearance in human form, is initiated as an act of great love by God for all people, unearned and undeserved.

Take a moment today to reflect on God's love for you, just as you are. Can you recall a particular time or situation in your life where you felt the nearness of God?

On a sticky note or an index card (or if you are feeling crafty, you can make a construction paper heart), jot a loving affirmation to hold for the day. Compose your own or select one of these reminders:

- You are where you need to be

- You are loved by God

- You are safe with God

Place this love note from God on your bathroom mirror, on the steering wheel of your car, or next to the kitchen sink as a gentle reminder of your belovedness.

Enfold me in your love, O God. Thank you for your compassion in the times of my unbelief. Thank you for the companionship that comes in places of belonging. Thank you for your grace for my regretful behavior. Remind me this day of your delight in me. Amen.

Luke 2:1–14

In those days a decree went out from Caesar Augustus that all the world should be registered. This was the first registration and was taken while Quirinius was governor of Syria. All went to their own towns to be registered.

Joseph also went from the town of Nazareth in Galilee to Judea, to the city of David called Bethlehem, because he was descended from the house and family of David. He went to be registered with Mary, to whom he was engaged and who was expecting a child.

While they were there, the time came for her to deliver her child. And she gave birth to her firstborn son and wrapped him in bands of cloth and laid him in a manger, because there was no place in the guest room.

Now in that same region there were shepherds living in the fields, keeping watch over their flock by night. Then an angel of the Lord stood before them, and the glory of the Lord shone around them, and they were terrified.

But the angel said to them, "Do not be afraid, for see, I am bringing you good news of great joy for all the people: to you is born this day in the city of David a Savior, who is the Messiah, the Lord. This will be a sign for you: you will find a child wrapped in bands of cloth and lying in a manger." And suddenly there was with the angel a multitude of the heavenly host, praising God and saying,

"Glory to God in the highest heaven,

and on earth peace among those whom he favors!"

Vastly Loved

GWEN

While they were there, the time came for her to deliver her child.
And she gave birth to her firstborn son and wrapped him in
bands of cloth and laid him in a manger, because there was
no place in the guest room.
—LUKE 2:6–7

Finally on our Advent journey we arrive at Christmas Day. After weeks of preparation in our hearts and in our homes, our energy now shifts to celebrating God's love incarnate. In a very humble setting yet surrounded by a loving mother and father, Jesus is born into an ordinary family. Amid the warmth of animal breath, he is wrapped in cloth and placed in a manger. This very earthy birth is set against the glory of God's celestial joy on display through the magnificence of an angel choir—so beautiful and otherworldly that the shepherds are terrified. Here in the Christmas story, we find a beautiful comingling of the sacred and the ordinary.

This is God's love and admonition on display for all to see. How much does God love us? Infinitesimally, exuberantly, completely, always. How does God demonstrate love? With a baby born into the loving warmth of family. With an angel choir singing praises. With shepherds coming to worship the Christ child. Throughout time and creation God has been present, and in the birth of Christ, God's presence is fully realized through incarnation. This is not so far removed from our own lives, which are mixtures of the everyday and the holy.

Our human expressions of love sometimes fall short. We get caught up in the small pains of life and in the huge, overwhelming drama of humankind. The injustices seem unceasing. Yet God's love is able to encompass it all. God's love is in the unfolding, vast sunrise. In the work of large organizations toward increasing food security and providing homes for the displaced. God's love is also present in the beautiful fingers and toes of a newborn child. In the small, everyday choices we make to forgive slights, to hold someone's hand, to pray for others.

Whether you are focusing on the big picture of God's love for the world or on the details of daily living, take time this week to notice how divine love shows up in your life. All of us are unique vessels for God's love to pour out into the world. There are as many different ways to share as there are different kinds of people.

Not surprisingly, God's creative love is on display in God's people. In your Christmas celebrations this week and as you interact with other people, be intentional about noticing how each person uniquely expresses God's love. How have those you encountered expressed God's love? How have you been able to love others well in your time together?

May our hearts be full of God's vast love now in Christmastide and beyond.

Holy, holy God, we humbly offer our work to you. May we be expressions of your love, which you demonstrated so completely in your Son, Jesus. Amen.

Pecan Tarts

GWEN

*C*hristmas often calls us home to the people we love. Throughout my childhood, our family traveled to my father's hometown for an annual celebration with his parents and siblings. Various traditional family foods were part of the celebration. Held in highest esteem by all the grandchildren, myself included, were the beautiful cookie plates. Each family brought something to add to the large platters, which were filled with an astounding variety of perfectly baked cookies.

When I pull my copy of *Favorite Community Recipes: White Horse Fire Company Auxiliary Cookbook* off the shelf, it is often to make pecan tarts. As I mix the ingredients, I remember the already and not yet of Advent. I think fondly about the Christmas Days spent in Pennsylvania with cousins (and large cookie platters). And I also feel the melancholic beauty we treasure in honoring others when they are no longer here. These memories are placed alongside the joy of creating a sweet, nutty treat to share with my family and friends who *are* present with me this Christmas season.

This cookbook is a treasured gift from my Aunt Mayme, who passed away December 7, 2000. On the cover is a picture of the White Horse Fire Department in Pennsylvania, which was located across the street from my aunt and uncle's house when I was growing up. My Aunt Mayme decorated her home in a special way; her kitchen included a cozy woodstove, and the rest of the house featured quilts and her teacup collection. And, perhaps most important, I felt warmly welcomed when our family visited. She also noticed that I loved to bake and gave me my very own cookbook. It was the first cookbook that was "mine" on the shelf in my mother's kitchen, and I still think of her when I use it today to make pecan tarts.

The Pecan Tarts recipe shared below is now a personal family favorite at Christmas time and, if they're not all gone before the official celebration, the tarts are added to my family's Christmas Day cookie platters.

PECAN TARTS

Ingredients

Crust

1⅛ cups all-purpose flour

½ cup (1 stick) cold butter, cubed

3-ounces cold cream cheese, cubed

Filling

1 cup lightly packed brown sugar

1 egg

2 tablespoons butter, melted

¼ teaspoon vanilla

¾ cup chopped pecans

Method

Preheat the oven to 350°F.

To make the crust, combine the flour, butter, and cream cheese in a medium bowl. With a fork, mix and press cream cheese and butter into the flour to form a coarse mixture, until the butter and cream cheese are about pea-sized pieces throughout the flour. Do not overmix. Press the dough into a large ball. Divide into 24 evenly sized balls. Press dough balls into greased mini muffin tins to form thick, pie-shaped crusts.

To make the filling, mix brown sugar, egg, butter, vanilla, and chopped pecans thoroughly in a large bowl. Fill mini muffin tins ⅔ full, using about a teaspoon of filling per tart. Bake for 20 to 25 minutes at 350°F. The edges of the crust should be slightly browned when fully baked.

Yields 24 mini tarts

A Sign for You

SHERAH-LEIGH

"Do not be afraid, for see, I am bringing you good news of great joy for all the people: to you is born this day in the city of David a Savior, who is the Messiah, the Lord. This will be a sign for you . . ."
—LUKE 2:10–12

I just want to know that God loves me," my client whispered through tears as we chatted by video message. My heart broke as I heard the grief and fear behind the words in our soul care conversation. As a pastor and spiritual director, I have borne witness to this kind of conversation in many settings. It's not an uncommon desire or challenge. Yet I long for the Spirit to show up! I, too, press on in prayer for signs of God's love to manifest to those who yearn for that assurance.

It's kind of surprising when I think about it. In this part of the Christmas story, an angel chorus shows up (which already must have been a miraculous and startling sight), and then proclaims the words which are so familiar to our ears: *this will be a sign for you* . . . . And if the wonder and spectacle of the angel's announcement wasn't enough, the chorus offers a sign of this promise and truth.

Indeed, what wondrous love God gave us in the birth of Jesus. Not only was this good news to those who were long awaiting a promised Messiah, but this was to be good news for all. Not only did Jesus' birth bring wonder and delight to Mary and Joseph, but also to those on the margins. This good news came to the shepherds who were pulling the night shift; these poor and pitied people were among the first to hear and know. And the good news came to magi, wise ones from far-off lands. God's love was for everyone.

Even when we logically assent to knowing the truth of God's love, it can be hard to embrace the reality with our whole being. What would it mean to experience God's love deep within your own heart? Perhaps you have felt a sense of failure for questioning God's love, care, or presence in your own life. Yet the angelic message in the Christmas story reminds us that it is human to need a sign. It is typical to look for ongoing reminders, to ask for reassurance.

The celebration of Christmas is a ritual touchstone of the divine love that is ours. The nativity is one sign. At times we need multiple signposts of God's kingdom to embrace the good news. That doesn't make us weak in our faith or somehow unworthy, but instead makes us fully human. God delights in reminding us of God's deep and unending love for us. God speaks to us through creation, through signs and wonders, through other people who offer words of comfort and wisdom, and most of all through the incarnation—Emmanuel, God with us.

O God, I long to sense your nearness, and to witness more signs of your love for me. Tune my heart to the whispers of your presence that surround me. May I see glimpses of you. Settle my heart in the steadfastness of your love. Amen.

Well Loved

SHERAH-LEIGH

In middle school, I always looked forward to sleepovers at my friend Katie's house. There we would spend hours listening to mainstream music CDs on repeat and look through teen magazines—contraband in my house. We would carefully fill in the answer bubbles for the various quizzes included, poring over the pronouncements about the type of friend you are, your smile style, or jewelry personality.

Some of us bristle at the idea of being boxed in. Even so, the wide range of personality typing systems and assessments (think Enneagram, Myers-Briggs, DISC, etc.) available and referenced both in social settings and in the business world signal the appeal of being known and identified in particular ways.

At one time, Gary Chapman's conception of the five love languages was quite popular.[7] Millions of people read his bestselling book to identify their penchant to prioritize physical touch, words of affirmation, quality time, gifts, or acts of service (the preferred Mennonite expression, I believe). While it is reductive and simplistic to think the experience of love can be fully explained using these simple categories, it helps to define a notion that can feel elusive. For many people, this framework concretizes the ways we attempt to offer and express love.

Set apart time for quiet processing either in your journal or through conversation with a friend. Consider the ways that you experience love in your life. Use these questions to prompt your thinking and shape your reflections.

- How do I experience God's love for me?

- What is true about God's love for me?

- What makes me feel well loved by people who are close to me?

- How do I demonstrate my love for others?

- What expectations do I need to release to experience love more deeply?

You demonstrate your love for me in many ways, O God. Thank you for the gift of your presence enfleshed in the nativity and now through the Spirit. The story of your work in the world and your words of comfort in scripture are my guide and companion. The signs of your love and provision that come through others in my community nurture and sustain me. May I love others as generously as you have loved me. Amen.

The Ministry of Availability

SHERAH-LEIGH

Midlife is where dreams go to die," I choked out as I wearily laid my head on the table between us. Gwen and I had each wound our way through opposite ends of the mountain range to meet at a coffee shop perched atop a steep and narrow side street in Morgantown, West Virginia.

Over pumpkin-spiced lattes we caught up on the latest life happenings. A few months earlier, my family had moved from the Shenandoah Valley to the heart of Amish country in Ohio. Committed to continuing writing together, Gwen and I had scheduled this midpoint meet-up as a chance to chat, write, and pack the comfort kits that we were promoting with our blog's upcoming Epiphany devotional series.

While we both loved and believed in our fledgling writing project, it seemed our personal passions and dreams were taking a backseat to the many other things happening in our lives. The previous two years had been difficult. We'd both weathered the COVID-19 pandemic, moved houses, and lost a parent-in-law after a period of decline. Regrouping from intense discernment, transitions, and grief, we were both feeling stretched between the demands of motherhood and the pressures of caring for aging parents.

In her book *Seasons of Family Life*, professor and author Wendy Wright describes the vocation of motherhood as the ministry of availability, which seems to be a true assessment of the work of parenthood.[8] Perhaps this insight holds significance more broadly. Is availability not also the call of Christian discipleship? Offering our presence and attention is a powerful way to show love to those whom we care about. At times we may do so more out of obligation than desire, true, but we have daily opportunities to give our energy and focus to those relationships nearest to us.

Mary's contribution to the miracle of Christmas (and the ongoing life, ministry, and impact of Jesus) was that of the ministry of availability. Her assent to the invitation of God and her nurture and care in birthing and raising Jesus demonstrate the sacred, ordinary work of tending to the people around us. Her greatest act of love was continuing to open herself, giving freely of her time and attention. And that is an invitation and opportunity that each one of us has, at every stage of life.

Consider how being present to what is (as it is right now) may be the greatest expression of love you can offer. How can you engage in the ministry of availability to those in your sphere of influence at work, at home, or in your community? How might this kind of attentive love bring healing, hope, and transformation in the situations near to your heart?

Of the many ways we can connect with God, the companionship of our community of believers is one that bears witness to our questions, trials, and pains. The presence of our soul friends demonstrates and embodies God's loving care for us in different seasons and situations. We have benefited from the ministry of availability of others—friends, family, and church communities. And no matter our present circumstances, we, too, can offer our prayerful attention to those we encounter each day.

Blessing to Love

GWEN

May we grasp
impossibly
the breadth of

God's Love

May we be transformed
miraculously
in the height of

God's Love

May we overflow
abundantly
filled with the depth of

God's Love

WEEK 6

Emmanuel

Ponder

SHERAH-LEIGH

Draw the blinds on the day.

Relax your body
Snuggle deep under covers

Breathe deeply
Slowly
Rhythmically

Rest
Release
Sleep
Integrate

Treasure
Dream
Imagine

Renew
Rise

It is a gift.

Familiar yet Fresh

SHERAH-LEIGH

Gwen and I share a love of books, so it was both obvious and imperative that I invite her to join the book club my sister and I were forming. However, it didn't take long to realize that while we shared the joy of reading, we didn't share the same taste in books or reading habits. One significant difference in our reading lives is that I do not care to reread books. With so many titles and an outrageously long to-be-read list, I am always ready to read the next title!

After a few years in pastoral ministry, though, I began to appreciate the value of rereading. While there is more scripture to explore and dissect than any congregation could manage in a year of worship services, the rhythm of the liturgical year brings us to familiar passages again and again. Just how many times can one find a new angle or insight on the same scripture story? Yet I am discovering the rich gift of scripture to hold new revelations time and again.

Part of the comfort of the Christmas season is its familiarity. The carols we sing, the traditions we engage, and the well-known, repeated words of the nativity story found in the Bible all contribute to the ritual and warmth experienced during the holidays.

When annual traditions are so close to our hearts, it can be difficult to see them differently or discover new insights. Yet each time we come to these beloved stories, we bring with us another year of experiences and perspectives. We are not the same hearer or participant that we were at five, fifteen, or thirty-two.

Mary's story had a different resonance the Advent that I was pregnant with my own son. I certainly was pondering things, hand resting on my swelling belly; I was filled with prayers of gratitude and petition for this new life and all that his arrival would surely change.

Joseph and Mary's flight to Egypt, along with all the anxieties and challenges the journey must have held for the holy family, moves my heart differently after sharing meals with refugee neighbors turned friends. Harsh political headlines cause more pain and distress when we understand the humanity and belovedness of those impacted by policies and persecution. And yet because the nativity text is so familiar, we may miss these kinds of connections if we don't stop to consider them afresh each year. We rely on our rote recitation of phrases and songs. We may neglect the comfort offered by the common themes of the season as we light the candles of the Advent wreath. We might fail to notice that one gift of Luke's gospel is how it collects stories from so many different people who were impacted by various parts of the Christmas story. Luke records the experiences of ordinary folks caught up in God's extraordinary actions. Mary, Joseph, Herod, Zechariah, Elizabeth, John, Simeon, Anna, the shepherds, and angels— each one gives us a window onto the impact of the incarnation on a wide variety of people.

The good tidings and great joy of the nativity is Emmanuel. It's easy to overlook the fresh power of this familiar truth. God has come to be with us in the flesh, as a baby. It is this "with-ness" that is at the heart of Christmas. Scripture reminds us that those who are caught up in the unfolding drama of the nativity also have a wide range of experiences; we are welcome regardless of the feelings stirred within us at this time of year. There is space for fear and great joy, for grief and wild hope.

We have journeyed through Advent, a time of preparation and waiting. And now, with the arrival of the Christ child, the long-awaited revolution is ramping up. God's presence and transforming power arrives in a new and unexpected way. The way of peace and love, the witness of Emmanuel, will turn things upside down. We participate in a world that has been forever changed by the incarnation.

Being With

SHERAH-LEIGH

It's the perfect job," I explained to my friends, who expressed both surprise and concern when I announced I was learning to milk cows at the neighboring farm. Animal husbandry certainly wasn't in my wheelhouse as a writer and pastor. "With the night shift, I won't miss out on anything and can still follow through with the other contract work I'm piecing together," I declared.

Of course there is no such thing as a *perfect* job, and soon the flaws in my plan revealed themselves. Perhaps the most unexpected, unintended consequence of my new work schedule was missing out on the bedtime routine.

Since my children are now in double digits, they are independent in their bedtime preparations, but they still submit to being tucked in. Occasionally, they request that I lay with them until they fall asleep. In the early years, those endless minutes of waiting for a child to give in to sleep, then slowly maneuvering out of their bed and across the floor, trying to avoid any creaks that would rouse them, were painstaking. I longed for personal space and time to do what I wished.

But as my children's bedtimes began to pass by without any connection point, I realized how sweet and sacred that time had been. Reviewing the day together, creating space for winding down, and submitting to the discipline of waiting in the quiet dark were all gifts I missed as I instead moved cows through the milking parlor.

As we celebrate the birth of Emmanuel this Christmas, we highlight the unique gift of God's incarnate presence among us, and we keep watch for the ways the Spirit companions us now.

Today, light a candle as a reminder of the nearness of God. Perhaps you will keep the candle on your desk while you work or use it as a centerpiece at the dinner table when you have your evening meal. When you reflect on the scripture for this week and its emphasis on the miracle and wonder of God with us in human form, consider the ways you are *with* God. How do you experience God's presence? How do you hold space for holy connections in the ordinary days and interactions with others?

Allow the warmth, light, and flame of the candle to be a reminder of God's nearness, comfort, and love.

Luke 2:15–20

When the angels had left them and gone into heaven, the shepherds said to one another, "Let us go now to Bethlehem and see this thing that has taken place, which the Lord has made known to us."

So they went with haste and found Mary and Joseph and the child lying in the manger.

When they saw this, they made known what had been told them about this child, and all who heard it were amazed at what the shepherds told them, and Mary treasured all these words and pondered them in her heart.

The shepherds returned, glorifying and praising God for all they had heard and seen, just as it had been told them.

Embodied Christ

GWEN

*The shepherds returned, glorifying and praising God
for all they had heard and seen.*
—LUKE 2:20

Our embodied existence includes times of great joy and times of suffering—both can even be wrapped into one experience. Sometimes my middle schooler will exclaim, "I am so sore!" after a particularly taxing game of soccer or a demanding physical education class. When I comment that perhaps he could slow down his movements and lessen the hurt afterward, he disagrees. He experiences such joy when exercising his physical body that to decrease his efforts seems impossible.

Our bodies speak to us every day. When I am hungry, or tired, or long to stretch my legs, I am hearing my body speak. Acknowledging our physical needs and caring for them also helps us become attuned to our spirits. Our bodies send us messages about our spiritual wellbeing. Recognizing that I am thirsty and then getting a drink can lead me to notice when my shoulders are tense. Recognizing that my body is holding tension can remind me to take a break from a stressful situation, or perhaps reveal that I am nervous and would benefit from taking deep breaths.

Embodied living is a beautiful gift from God. Learning to listen thoughtfully to the messages from our God-created human form can increase our awareness of our whole being. And listening to our spirit and acknowledging our humanity can draw us closer to God.

The wonderful, holy event of God coming among us is the story and the promise retold each year during the Christmas season. God created us in human form. Christ came as Emmanuel, God with us. Our bodies are holy and cracked vessels that are able to carry out God's kingdom work in the world; the shepherds most likely had their faults, yet they are some of the first humans to respond to Christ's birth by "glorifying and praising God" (Luke 2:20). They physically ran toward God and visited the Christ child.

As we turn our bodies toward the new year, may we reflect on the holiness of embodied life and listen to the messages our bodies send us. May we thank God that our bodies allow us physical expression of a spiritual existence. May we consider the gift it is that the advent of Christ happened in a body. And may we thank God again that each of us has been given the gift of a finite, beautiful, holy, created body.

Emmanuel, thank you for coming to be God with us. May we step joyfully into the new year feeling thankful for Your continued presence with us on the journey. Amen.

Christmas Fruit Salad

GWEN

Over the years, we have learned to be flexible with how our family celebrates Christmas. My father's family Christmas gathering had many traditions associated with it, including strict adherence to gathering on December 25. But as my siblings and I married and moved to various locations, it became a tradition for my immediate family to gather and celebrate the week following Christmas instead. This gathering developed its own traditions, including stockings stuffed with helpful kitchen gadgets, earrings, and hand tools for the adults, and flashlights and small, wind-up toys for the children. For many years my mom graciously hosted a family-style banquet that my children grew to love. They looked forward to their grandma's steaming, masterfully seasoned mashed potatoes and gravy along with all the other fixings. Each generation found its own rhythms and looked forward to unique ways of celebrating together.

When I was in my late forties, our family traditions shifted again. My parents moved next door to me in a downsized cottage, and while my mom was happy to help with planning the holiday celebration, the venue moved from her house to mine. Once I became responsible for the meal, I realized that I would need to create new traditions, ones that would work for my family and my siblings' families. I quickly became aware of the hours my mom had spent over the years making Christmas as perfect and meaningful as she could, despite our various dietary needs and general opinions about family traditions. I learned I definitely wasn't my mother! Not only did I not have the same culinary skills, I lacked the time and patience to orchestrate gatherings like hers.

When Sherah-Leigh and I were gathering recipes for this project, I recalled the delicious fruit salad with pudding that we ate at my grandmother's

134

home many years ago. As I described the memory to my family, my mom said, "Your Aunt Liz and I came up with that one together. People weren't big fans of just plain fruit salad, so we added pudding."

This story made me smile. I imagined my mom and her sisters-in-law trying to design a menu that would be nutritious and appeal to the many hungry nieces and nephews gathering for the annual Christmas meal. They had to reinterpret their family's traditions as the celebration grew and more people were added to the table. What I had thought of as something that had "always" been a part of Christmas dinner at Grandma's had actually been added taking into account the expanding family's palate.

I have adapted the original recipe for this fruit salad, since we now have so many more fresh fruits available at Christmas than we did when I was a young child. I also changed some elements for the sake of convenience. This recipe retains the spirit of the delicious and refreshing dessert from my childhood memory, and the beauty of fruit salad is that you can also tailor it to meet your family's likes and dislikes.

CHRISTMAS DAY FRUIT SALAD

This recipe makes a very large bowl of fruit salad. It is perfect if you are hosting a hungry crowd. However, it doesn't keep well, so if you have leftovers, eat them quickly! If you want to make a smaller fruit salad, decrease the amount of fruit you combine and mix in only part of the pudding instead of the whole batch. The extra pudding can be stored in the refrigerator and enjoyed as a snack by itself or with your favorite pudding accompaniment.

Ingredients

Pudding

1½ tablespoons cornstarch

1½ cups milk, divided

¼ cup granulated sugar

1 egg, well beaten

1½ tablespoons butter

¼ teaspoon vanilla

1 cup whipped cream or nondairy whipped topping

Mixed Fruit

1 (15-ounce) can mandarin oranges, drained

2 cups halved grapes

1 pint fresh blueberries

1 cup canned pineapple tidbits (do not include liquid)

2 red apples, chopped

1 (15-ounce) can of sliced peaches, drained and chopped into bite-size
   pieces

1 large ripe banana (reserve for later)

Method

To make the pudding, mix the cornstarch in ½ cup milk and set aside. In a medium saucepan on the stove, combine the remaining 1 cup milk, sugar, egg, and butter. Whisk to combine and begin heating mixture over medium heat. Whisk in the reserved milk with cornstarch, and continue cooking and stirring until thickened to a pudding consistency, about 3 to 4 minutes. Stir continuously with a whisk or wooden spoon while the mixture thickens.

Remove the pan from the heat and add vanilla. Set aside to cool.

When the pudding is cool, fold in the whipped cream or nondairy whipped topping. Store the pudding in a sealed container in the refrigerator until serving.

To make the mixed fruit, prepare each fruit component as indicated (the draining step is important), except the banana; then mix the fruits together in a large bowl. If you notice liquid pooling in the bottom of the bowl, drain it again. Store the fruit mixture in the refrigerator until you are ready to serve.

Immediately before serving, slice and add banana to the salad. Gently stir in the cooled pudding with the fruit salad.

Yields 12 or more servings

Treasuring and Pondering

SHERAH-LEIGH

And Mary treasured all these words
and pondered them in her heart.

—LUKE 2:19

"Would you still say yes if you had known?" The stranger's brown eyes met mine as he approached me after the worship service. "If you had known that things would turn out like this, would you have still said yes to pastoral ministry?"

I was providing pulpit supply for a friend and preached on the account of Jesus calling his disciples. In the message, I had woven in my own story of being called to ministry, reflecting on some of the things I gave up to pursue what I believed God was inviting me to. But it had been a challenging sermon to preach because it came in a season of employment upheaval. My most recent ministry assignment had ended painfully. My next vocational move was unknown. Sometimes the sermon we preach or the counsel we give is the message our own heart most needs to receive.

"Would you do it all over again?" This question haunted me in the days after speaking to the congregation. I found myself wishing for the chance to offer a better response than a fumbling, "It's complicated, but probably yes . . ."

In this week's lectionary passage, the shepherds arrive and confirm what Mary and Joseph already believe about their son. But instead of outwardly expressing relief or jubilation, Mary ponders and treasures all that is said. While we most often think of receiving confirmation as a blessing, it seems that Mary's experience of this particular prophecy, calling, and now fulfilment also stirred questions and perhaps concerns.

Humans long for signs, wonders, and miraculous intervention. Yet we never want to be in the place of needing such rescue. And when the desired relief comes, it is rarely as neatly packaged as we imagined it would be.

The refrain of *fear not* reminds us that being chosen by God can be equally harrowing as it is honoring; just as scary as sacred. Perhaps following after God is always a risky proposition because it requires us to maintain faith and trust, a posture of hope.

Celebrating the incarnation is another reminder that the divine gift is God's presence with and among us. Even when we have signs and assurances, we still may wonder: *How can this be? What will it mean?* Usually, we know only in part. Yet we see in Mary that this incomplete knowledge and contemplation is a holy response. God is with us in our worries and wonderings. God is near, inviting, equipping, and guiding. What signs of God's presence can you treasure and ponder this week?

In my fear, may your comforting Spirit be near, O God. In my wondering, may I experience a sense of peace. In the midst of the unfolding journey ahead, may I notice your presence surrounding me. Amen.

Embracing Humanity

SHERAH-LEIGH

What if the invitation of the incarnation is to be *more* human?

In many spaces of religious conversation and nurture, the emphasis is placed on the sin nature of humanity, of our need for transformation. We examine and revere Jesus' divinity, striving in our discipleship toward holy perfection. Throughout church history, the writings preserved and often upheld are those that eschew humanity and long for divinity.

But what if we embraced our humanity? What would it mean to learn to live well within the confines of finitude? Consider what the God-with-us message of human flesh, growing and aging with proximity to others, might mean for the goodness of your season of life.

- What would it mean for me to make peace with the reality that our earthly time has limits?

- How can I appreciate (instead of begrudge) the limitations of my physical body today?

- What sensation, movement, or ability can I be particularly thankful for on this day?

As you reflect on these ideas, you may choose to write or speak a prayer of appreciation for your body and the physical pleasures of your human experience. Invite the Spirit's tender provision for the places of pain and disappointment that exist in your body. Listen for the response of the Spirit to your words of gratitude and grief.

Creator God, you formed humanity from the dust of the earth, breathed into us your Spirit, and declared our bodies good. At times the wounds within your precious creation cause us to forget our goodness. At times the losses we feel because of aging and the diseases of our time become our focus. Yet you chose to join in the limits of the human form. You know the pleasures and pains of an embodied existence. Today, may I take delight in the goodness of being human. Amen.

God with Us

GWEN

On my son's eighteenth birthday, I unconsciously backed out of a photo my husband was taking. "Where are you going?" he asked. Only later was I able to examine my reaction. I was backing out of the photo because I was self-conscious about how my body would look in the picture.

How many times have you heard someone say, "Well, I need to lose a few pounds," or "I don't like the way I look in this outfit" in response to a compliment? Have you ever thought, "If my [insert body part/physical feature] were [insert desired difference] then I would be beautiful?" In a world where information is at our fingertips and pictures are easily filtered or photoshopped, the pressure to transform and shape our bodies in a certain way is tremendous. If we use the unrealistic standard we find on the internet, our own bodies will always measure below.

Genesis 2:7 retells, "Then the LORD God formed man from the dust of the ground." The author recounts God's actions as purposeful, like a sculptor molding clay. Acknowledging God's hand in the making of our bodies inspires new respect and kindness for our physical selves. We were not created to last forever, nor to be perfect physical specimens, nor in the same way as anyone else. God clearly and happily created us as individuals in all our humanness.

God knows about my sweet tooth. God understands how midlife weight tends to move to the middle. God loves my friend's nose, the church elder's wrinkles, and whatever body part you are convinced is flawed. God delights in the diversity of our bodies. God sees our uniqueness and rejoices.

Have you ever wondered what Jesus looked like? As a newborn, was his head pointy? Did he have baby acne? Was he colicky? What does it actually mean that Jesus was fully God and fully human? Does the God part mean Jesus had a perfect body? What does a perfect body look like, anyway? Probably not what we imagine.

The fact that God came to dwell with us as a person shows God's great love and compassion for humanity in general and also for the form in which God created us—bodies! Beautiful human bodies!

While we don't know exactly what Jesus' body looked like, we do see many examples in the New Testament of how Jesus took care of his own body and the bodies of others he encountered. Jesus healed the sick from physical and mental anguish, and he fed thousands of people. Through his miraculous actions, he acknowledged our bodily circumstance. Jesus rested when he was tired and cried when he was sad. He lived in his body, and he took care of his human form.

God sent Jesus, Emmanuel—literally meaning the divine embodied—so that we could have an example of how to navigate the world's simultaneous holiness and imperfection. Jesus cared so deeply and gently for the bodies of others and his own human body. He honored both the needs of others and his own limits by spending time in solitude, expressing the full range of emotions (including anger and sadness), and joyfully engaging in friendship and community life. His example is a marvelous template for us to follow in how to treat our own bodies and the bodies of others with kindness and respect.

Consider how embracing your human body as it is now would bring joy to your life. How might loving the body God gave you change the way you experience food, exercise, and being human? How can you extend this gracious attitude toward others in your daily interactions?

What a joy to know that we have this embodied experience, a true gift from God, in common with Jesus! What an honor to take into the new year: a body created, full of uniqueness, a blessing—even in its imperfection—for our current journey.

Blessing My Body

GWEN

In my whole body,
be present, Lord.

My hands
working,
working out your purpose.

My legs
walking,
walking toward your kingdom.

My torso
turning,
turning to see your face.

Christ
Emmanuel
God with us
in a body.

In my whole body
be working, walking, and turning
me, Lord,
on my way to you.

Amen

Conclusion

SHERAH-LEIGH

*T*he house always feels a bit empty when the dust settles from holiday festivities. I dread taking down the tree, matching ornaments to boxes, and carefully winding up strands of lights. I leave the window candles on display a few weeks more. January in northeastern Ohio can be quite bleak, and the cozy glow gracing the front windows is comforting and inviting.

But the exhale of Christmas cheer, the blank spaces that appear now that the furniture is returned to its rightful place and the garlands are tucked away until next December, ushers in a fresh start of sorts. Just as Advent gives way to Christmas, which yields to the celebration of Epiphany, so too our hearts have made the journey from preparation and anticipation into celebration. Now we gaze toward something new.

The capstone of the Christmas season in the liturgical calendar is Epiphany: a church festival commemorating the coming of the magi. When these wise ones from the East encounter the Christ child, their response is overwhelming joy. We celebrate the illuminating moment of discovery and realization as they encounter the divine. During this experience, these kings develop an intuitive grasp of something—*an epiphany*. And so they change course. They go home by another way (see Matthew 2:1–12).

As Christmastide concludes and we move into a new year, we hope that you have encountered the divine in fresh ways and that you have had an epiphany: seeing the sacred in the ordinary and noticing the Spirit's presence in the special events and celebrations of the past weeks.

May you be changed by the practices, insights, and experiences of this Advent and Christmas, crossing the threshold into a new year with hope and joy.

May the wonder of God incarnate linger around you as you pack up the Christmas trimmings.

May you be full of the knowledge of God, and may God's presence continue to companion you in the coming year.

Acknowledgments

For us, writing is first and foremost a spiritual practice. We are so grateful for our *Some Comfort and Joy* community that has found meaning and been nurtured with our words in the world. Your engagement and encouragement have been a blessing to us!

We are also thankful for the Herald Press team who have made a dream come true: Amy Gingerich, Laura Leonard Clemens, Elisabeth Ivey, Sara Versluis, Joe Questel, LeAnn Hamby, Merrill Miller, Alyssa Bennett Smith, Rachel Martens, Eden Fisher, and Ardell Stauffer. Your vision, care, and expertise have been a gift.

And to our generous and brave recipe testers: Debbie Brunk, Tina Burkhart, Carissa Gredler, Maren Hange, Beth Falb, Moriah Hurst, Susan Huyard, Callie Janoff, Jolene Jaquet, Judy King, Laura Lehman, Mac McArthur-Fox, Lois Maust, Erin Ramer, Bonita Seely, Julie Shiflet, Jen and Mara Steiner, Karla Stoltzfus-Detweiler, and Miriam Zehr. Thank you for sharing in our excitement and helping us to translate our family traditions in ways that others can enjoy!

We would be skipping over the obvious if we did not take a moment to acknowledge the joy of coauthoring a book with a friend. You can picture the authors here hugging and celebrating the publication of this book!

FROM GWEN

The creation of this book required many trips down memory lane. I am thankful to my parents for the rich traditions you passed on to me and that I found on these journeys. My Amish and Mennonite roots run deep spiritually and culturally, and I am grateful to be the recipient of this heritage. If that were not enough, your encouraging words have buoyed me many times as I worked on my dream of being an author.

I am thankful to be writing at a time when Christian women authors are finding their voices and reclaiming, reevaluating, and proclaiming their faith. Reading and listening to many powerful women express their faith has shaped my own journey, and I am grateful.

To my large and amazing extended Lantz, Stoltzfus, and Ramer families—thank you. I have the overflowing blessing of many aunts, uncles, and cousins. You have given me words of encouragement and share in our numerous and sometimes quirky family roots.

Randy, Callie, Karla, and Nathan, I am blessed to have you as siblings. Your creative journeys and hopeful words give me courage. I hope seeing the family traditions recorded here brings you joy.

Thank you to Joel and Andrew. Thank you for allowing me space to travel away in my mind, and for having no trouble at all imagining your mom as an author. Doug, thank you for accepting me as my authentic self and for your unapologetic, trailblazing example in following and realizing dreams. You're my guys and I love you!

FROM SHERAH-LEIGH

I am indebted to the congregation that first called me pastor and was the testing ground for many of these ideas. Thank you for allowing me to practice and refine my craft in public.

My first readers, cheerleaders, and polo pals: Dawn Monger, Beth Hofstetter Falb, and Jolene Jaquet. Everyone deserves friends like you. I am where I am because of your confidence and encouragement.

I do not take for granted the legacy and rootedness that the Risser and Zehr families have provided for me and the warm welcome and traditions I've gained from the Gerbers. To my dear pastor-parents, Doug and Miriam, and sisters, Charissa and Maria, who formed me: I am grateful our stories are forever entwined. I hope these reflections honor our shared experiences well.

The reflections and practices in this book only exist because of the generosity of my own sweet family and the crucible of our beautiful life together. Anna and Titus, you continue to show me the sacred in the ordinary, and I'm delighted to be your mother; BJ, your unwavering support and sacrifice means more than words could ever express. Thank you, thank you, thank you.

Additional Resources

Basic Sweet Bread Dough

This family recipe is the base for my (Sherah-Leigh) mom's famous cinnamon rolls that we enjoyed each Sunday morning. The dough works well for any sweet bread that you want to make. While my mom mixed all the ingredients with a wooden spoon and kneaded the dough by hand, this dough will also come together easily in a stand mixer. Just be sure not to overwork the dough or the baked bread will not be as tender. When the flour is well incorporated, turn the dough out onto a lightly floured surface and complete the kneading with your hands.

Ingredients
  1½ cups (12 ounces) lukewarm water, divided
  ¼ cup plus ½ teaspoon granulated sugar
  1 tablespoon granulated yeast
  ½ tablespoon salt
  ¼ cup vegetable oil
  4½ cups all-purpose flour

Method
Mix together ½ cup lukewarm water, ½ teaspoon granulated sugar, and yeast in a large bowl. Stir until yeast is dissolved. Let the mixture sit for 10 minutes.

When the yeast is frothy, add in the additional 1 cup water and ¼ cup sugar; then add the salt and vegetable oil. Incrementally add in the flour (about 1 cup at a time), mixing until well combined.

On a lightly floured countertop, knead the dough until smooth, about 3 minutes. Place kneaded dough in a greased bowl. Cover the bowl loosely with plastic wrap or a clean kitchen towel and allow the dough to rise at room temperature until doubled, about two hours. When doubled, the dough is ready to shape as a loaf, make into Star Bread (recipe is on page 55), cinnamon rolls, or use as the base for other sweet bread and roll recipes.

Chocolate Divinity Candy

This old-fashioned candy was often found on my (Gwen) grandmother Ramer's tiered Christmas cookie and fruit plate. She covered empty food cans with aluminum foil to place between plates with the largest plate on the bottom. Fresh fruit filled the bottom plate, the next layer often held cookies and nuts, and the final and smallest plate at the top held chocolate divinity candy.

Chocolate divinity candy can be used as a chocolate fudge base to mix in any of your favorite flavors. The recipe below adds cranberry, coconut, and pecans for a distinctive Christmastime mix. However, Grandmother Ramer usually added walnuts to her chocolate divinity candy. You can create your own complex chocolate fudge mix or use the more traditional 1 cup chopped nuts.

Ingredients

2 egg whites
2 cups granulated sugar
½ cup cold water
½ cup light corn syrup
3 tablespoons cocoa powder
1 teaspoon vanilla
pinch salt
½ cup sweetened shredded coconut
½ cup dried cranberries
24 pecan halves

Method

For best results, separate the egg whites from the yolks while the eggs are still cold from the refrigerator. Then allow the separated egg whites to come to room temperature.

Using a hand mixer with the whisk attachment, beat the room temperature egg whites to stiff peaks in a large bowl.

Boil sugar, water, and corn syrup over medium heat stirring frequently until a drop of the mixture in cold water turns brittle. This stage is reached after approximately 5 minutes at a rolling boil, or until the mixture reads 270°F on a candy thermometer. Remove the syrup mixture from the heat.

Add cocoa powder, vanilla, and salt to the peaked egg whites, but do not mix. Wait to incorporate these ingredients until the syrup is added.

Slowly pour the hot syrup mixture over the egg whites, cocoa, salt, and vanilla, beating on low while you pour. Continue beating the mixture on medium-high until it is creamy and holds its shape. This takes 4 to 5 minutes.

To test if the chocolate divinity candy is ready, try dipping a spoonful of the mixture onto a plate. If the mixture holds its shape as it cools, it is ready for the next step. Another indicator is that when the beaters are lifted from the mixture, it clings to the beaters and begins to harden as it cools.

Quickly stir in the sweetened shredded coconut and dried cranberries (or whatever nut and dried fruit combination you prefer).

Pour the chocolate divinity candy into a greased 9 x 5-inch loaf pan. Smooth the top with an icing spatula. Press pecan halves into the still-warm candy at intervals so that you will have one pecan half per candy square (in rows of 4 pecans by 6 pecans). Allow fudge to cool and then cut into small squares. For smooth cutting, use a sharp knife warmed with hot water. Store candy at room temperature in an airtight container.

Yields 2 dozen candies

Christmas Sweet Bread (Stollen)

The sweet, yeasted dough, combined with the festive-colored citron and lemon flavor, bakes into a delicious and extra special holiday breakfast treat. Of course, you can use raisins instead of citron or experiment with other dried fruits, depending on your family's preferences.

Ingredients

Dough

1 recipe Basic Sweet Bread Dough (page 152)
1 tablespoon grated lemon rind
½ cup sliced almonds
¼ cup citron

Glaze

1 cup powdered sugar
2 tablespoons lemon juice
1 to 2 tablespoons water

Method

Follow the Basic Sweet Bread Dough recipe on page 152 or another favorite. After the sweet bread dough has risen according to the recipe's instructions, turn the dough out onto a lightly floured counter. Gradually knead in lemon rind, almonds, and citron, working with about one-third of the ingredients at a time.

Shape the dough into a large horizontal oval, about ¼-inch thick. Then fold the dough almost in half (the right side should be slightly short of the left side) on the short halfway line. As your loaf rises it will have a stacked affect. Place folded loaf on a buttered baking sheet. Cover with a damp tea towel and let rise until doubled.

While the shaped loaf rises, preheat oven to 375°F. Bake for 35 minutes, or until the bread is lightly brown on the top. Remove the pan from the oven and set it on a wire rack to cool.

As the bread is cooling, mix together the powdered sugar, lemon juice, and water in a small bowl until you reach your desired consistency. Drizzle the glaze over the bread while it is still warm.

Yields 1 loaf (10 servings)

Festive Beverages

Gwen and I (Sherah-Leigh) have shared many conversations over steaming mugs. Whether in a local coffee shop or in one of our homes, we often indulge in beverages that feature seasonal flavors. If you are snowed in or hosting a friend, here are some ways to make your own version of common coffee house favorites.

COFFEE SHOP BEVERAGE FLAVOR MATRIX

This simple chart can help you craft your favorite coffee house drink at home. Where the chart says "spice," you can add ¼ teaspoon of pumpkin pie spice, cinnamon, or other warming spice (or seasonal spice blend) to change up the flavor profile. If you prefer espresso to brewed coffee, you can substitute 1 espresso shot instead.

	Warm (or Steamed) Milk	Brewed Coffee	Spice	Honey or Simple Syrup*	Cocoa
Brewed Coffee	to taste	8 ounces	¼ teaspoon	to taste	--
Latte	¾ cup	8 ounces	¼ teaspoon	1 teaspoon	--
Mocha	¾ cup	8 ounces	¼ teaspoon	1 teaspoon	½ teaspoon

Homemade Peppermint Mocha

Although I (Sherah-Leigh) take my coffee black, I am always tempted to upgrade my morning caffeine to something a little more special in winter. The pleasant scent and fresh kick of peppermint added to a classic mocha is a simple way to bring the familiar flavors of the season into an ordinary day.

Ingredients
  1 cup (8 ounces) strong brewed coffee
  2 ounces milk
  2 tablespoons Grandma Mim's Homemade Hot Chocolate Mix
      (page 159)
  Peppermint simple syrup*

Method
Brew strong coffee

  In a small saucepan, warm milk over medium heat and mix with brewed coffee.

  Add homemade hot chocolate mix (or 1 tablespoon of chocolate syrup if you have that on hand instead). Add peppermint simple syrup* to desired sweetness.

*Simple syrup is made by heating equal parts sugar and water until sugar is fully dissolved and then allowing the syrup to cool. To make peppermint simple syrup, add a crushed candy cane into the simple syrup, stirring gently until the candy cane melts. Store simple syrup in a glass container with a lid; it will keep in the refrigerator for a few weeks.

Grandma Mim's Homemade Hot Chocolate Mix

Starting in high school, my sisters and I (Sherah-Leigh) developed a tradition of watching Christmas movies together during winter break. When I went off to college, that time together became more sacred as I didn't visit home during the semesters. Over the years, our list of movies has evolved. It's fun to share with my own children movies that I have been watching for decades. For my son, an essential part of the Christmas movie watching tradition is having a mug of homemade hot chocolate with a candy cane stirrer. This recipe from my mom makes a large batch of mix that our family uses throughout the winter.

Ingredients

5⅓ cups powdered milk

2 cups chocolate powdered drink mix (such as Nesquik), or 2 cups cocoa powder plus ¼ cup granulated sugar

¾ cup powdered coffee creamer

½ cup powdered sugar

Method

In a large bowl, combine all the ingredients with a whisk until well mixed. Store in a large, airtight container for up to six months.

To make hot chocolate: Use 3 tablespoons of mix per 1 cup hot water or warm milk. Stir the mix into liquid and serve with marshmallows. Add a candy cane for a peppermint twist!

Yields 45 servings

Mulled Cider

Not only is mulled cider a festive drink to serve to loved ones, it fills the house with a wonderful, spicy scent when warmed in a slow cooker.

3 quarts apple cider
1 teaspoon ground cinnamon
½ teaspoon ground allspice
½ teaspoon ground cloves
¼ teaspoon salt
3 or 4 lemon (thin) slices (to float on top)

Combine all the ingredients in a slow cooker set on low. Allow to cook for about two hours. Serve when hot.*

*If you are short on time, you can also warm the cider quickly in a pan on the stovetop and let it simmer until serving. It can also be poured in a slow cooker set on low to keep it warm after being heated quickly on the stove top.

Yields 12 (8-ounce) servings

Slow Cooker Cheddar Broccoli Soup

The teachers in my (Sherah-Leigh's) life use the term "Sunday scaries" to refer to the particular dread that can appear at the end of the weekend. To offset that unpleasant feeling, my family developed a tradition of having dinner with our neighbor friends. When the daylight was short, we would corral our kids to play together inside someone's home while the adults talked and the soup simmered. This simple, delicious soup makes a filling crowd pleaser.

Ingredients
½ a yellow onion, finely chopped
¼ cup (½ stick) butter, melted
2 cups chicken stock
2 cups chopped broccoli florets (fresh or frozen)
1 cup sliced or shredded carrots
¼ cup all-purpose flour
2 cups 2% milk*
2 cups shredded sharp cheddar cheese
Salt and pepper, to taste

Method
In a slow cooker, add the onion, butter, chicken stock, broccoli, and carrots. Cook on low for 4 to 6 hours, until the vegetables are soft.

About 30 minutes before serving, in a small bowl, whisk together the flour and milk* until smooth. Add the flour mixture to the slow cooker and stir to combine; continue cooking for 20 minutes.

Using an immersion hand blender, carefully puree the soup to your preferred thickness. Add in cheddar cheese, stirring to combine until the cheese is completely melted. Season to taste with salt and pepper.

*Whole milk, cream, or sour cream may be substituted for part or all of the milk to create a thicker broth.

Yields 6 to 8 servings

Wheatie Balls

I (Sherah-Leigh) only began to make Christmas candies under the tutelage of my mother-in-law. Now, these and other dipped goodies are my main contribution to the Christmas dessert spreads. My sister found a silicon melting pot which has made dipping (and cleanup) so much easier.

Ingredients

- 1 cup (2 sticks) butter, softened
- 2 cups peanut butter
- 3¾ cups powdered sugar
- 12 cups flake cereal (such as Wheaties), crushed
- 2 pounds coating chocolate or chocolate melting wafers (milk, dark, or a combination of both)

Method

In a large bowl, combine the butter, peanut butter, powdered sugar, and cereal until well mixed and free of clumps.

Using a cookie scoop or tablespoon, divide the dough into small, uniform portions, rolling each by hand to smooth into balls that are approximately the diameter of a quarter and no larger than a golf ball.

Place dough balls onto a parchment-lined baking sheet. Chill in the freezer for 15 to 20 minutes.

In the top of a double boiler or melting pot, melt the coating chocolate. (The coating chocolate can also be melted in the microwave, but to avoid burning, heat in short increments of 15 to 20 seconds and stir well between each time in the microwave.)

Remove the tray of dough balls from the freezer. Using a fork or skewer, dip each of the dough balls into the melted chocolate, turning until completely coated. Return dipped balls to the parchment-lined baking sheet and allow the chocolate to harden.

Wheatie Balls will keep in the freezer for up to 3 months.

Yields approximately 6 dozen

Recipe Index

How to Adapt for Small Groups

This book grew out of our blog writing venture at SomeComfortAndJoy .com. Drawn by our pithy and practical reflections, our community of readers appreciates the ways we help each other notice the sacred in the ordinary. While this book was written for individual use, it can also be adapted to be utilized as a guide for conversation in small groups or adult Christian education classes.

One of the core values of Anabaptism is community, and that manifests in a variety of ways. We believe and trust that each person has access to God, and that our discipleship journeys are enriched by the sharing, insight, and accountability gained from living and worshiping together. We expect the Spirit will enrich your experience of the reflections and practices in this book when used in community as well.

A suggested weekly format follows.

WELCOME

It is important to create a warm and inviting space for conversation regardless of group size or setting. You are welcome to adapt this guide in a variety of ways, but we believe that leading with a consistent and recognizable rhythm for your session together will help people to be more engaged.

As people settle in to your meeting time, make sure that everyone is acquainted with one another. In addition to sharing names, it may be helpful to ask everyone to respond to a simple question about their week. This will allow people to connect and shift gears to the time and space, and hearing everyone's voice initially will increase conversation and participation later in the session.

Each week, briefly preview the format of the time together so that people know what to expect. Many people are busy, particularly in the Advent season, so this guide doesn't assume or require any preparation to participate.

CONNECTING WITH THE WEEKLY THEME

Each week of Advent (and Christmas) has an overarching theme that we have threaded throughout the various devotional elements. To focus the discussion, invite participants to reflect on and share their responses to the listed theme question (see page 166). Following that discussion, you may choose to read one of the two theme reflections from the week.

CONNECTING WITH SCRIPTURE

Each week features a scripture text, chosen from the lectionary that tells part of the Christmas story. One helpful practice for engaging with scripture is a form of reading known as *lectio divina*. This refers to a prayerful, reflective time spent with a particular scripture text. It is an invitation to connect the ancient words with the current context of your life and experience more than a scholarly examination of the passage.

Read the week's text aloud three times, allowing for a few minutes of silence between each reading. The same translation may be used each of the three times or different participants could read different Bible versions for each of the readings.

Invite reflection and sharing after the final time of listening. Questions for conversation could include:

- What stood out to you when you heard the text?

- If you've heard this text before, what impressed you in a new way?

- What questions arise as you read the text?

- What part of the text connects with something in your own life?

- How do you see this week's theme present in this text?

INVITATION TO PRACTICE

Read the invitation to spiritual practice for the week. Depending on the activity, you can lead the group to experience it in the moment. Or, if it is more appropriate for your group, invite participants to share their reflections about previous experiences with the practice and potential commitments for implementing or experimenting with the practice in the coming week.

INVITATION TO REFLECT

Share the invitation for reflection from the week's readings. Allow for a few moments of quiet reflection. Give participants an opportunity to share their own responses to the reflection questions, allow them to draw connections between the theme, scripture text, and their own experiences.

BLESSING

Take a few minutes for participants to share prayer requests. Offer a closing prayer for the group to cover the concerns and joys shared, ending with the blessing for the week.

EXAMPLE SMALL GROUP TIME OUTLINE

Below is an example outline of a small group time using the elements explained above with content in place for "Week 1: Preparation" from the book. Each week, this format can be used and updated with the correlating content from the designated week.

Example: Week 1

Welcome

Connecting with the Theme: **Preparation**
    Reflect:

- How did your family get ready for Christmas when you were a child?

- How does your family prepare today?

- What is a treasured Christmas memory from any time in your life?

    Read: Reluctant Preparation and/or Good in the Present

Connecting with Scripture:
    Read: Luke 1:26–38 using the *lectio divina* method (see page 165).
    Reflect:

- What stood out to you when you heard the text?

- If you've heard this text before, what impressed you in a new way?

- What questions arise as you read the text?

- What part of the text connects with something in your own life?

- How do you see this week's theme present in this text?

Invitation to Practice
    Read: Gathering Evergreens

Invitation to Reflect
    Read: Releasing Expectations

Blessing
    Read: Blessing for the Waiting

Connecting with the Theme: Weekly Questions

Here are suggested discussion questions to prompt individual reflection and group sharing based on the weekly theme. Feel free to choose from the list or add your own.

Week 1: Preparation

- How did your family get ready for Christmas when you were a child?

- How does your family prepare today?

- What is a treasured Christmas memory from any time in your life?

Week 2: Hope

- Does your family have (or has your family had) any traditions that particularly evoke hope for you during the Advent and Christmas seasons? What are or were they?

- In the Hope Haikus, Gwen describes things that give her hope. What are some things that give you hope?

- When have you felt hopeless? What helped you recover a sense of hope?

- What are you hopeful for in the coming weeks?

Week 3: Joy

- How would you define "joy"?

- Do you think joy and happiness are different? Why or why not?

- How have you experienced joy in the past week?

Week 4: **Peace**

- Do you associate peace with the Advent and Christmas seasons? Why or why not?

- Why do you think peace is such a popular theme in holiday songs?

- Do you think peace is something to strive for or avoid? Why?

Week 5: **Love**

- When you reflect on the biblical Christmas story, is there a person in particular who helps you think of God's love in a new way? If so, who is it and why?

- Over the course of our lives, we experience times when life is moving along with few problems and other times when life is full of distress or frustration. Can you think of a time when God's love felt close to you? Or far away?

- What is a particular memory you have of feeling loved?

Week 6: **Emmanuel**

- What do you think Jesus looked like? Why? Does it help you to imagine Jesus having a physical human body?

- Have you had a time in your life when you experienced, in a surprising or memorable way, the presence of God with you?

- Why do you think our culture is so preoccupied with how our human forms should look?

Notes

1 Wilda C. Gafney, *A Women's Lectionary for the Whole Church: A Multi-Gospel Single-Year Lectionary* (New York: Church Publishing, 2021).

2 "Social Trauma and Public Spirituality: A Womanist Relational Ethic of Spiritual Practice," in *Kaleidoscope*, edited by Ineda Pearl Adesanya (New York: Church Publishing, 2019), 157.

3 Catherine Price, *The Power of Fun: How to Feel Alive Again* (New York: The Dial Press, 2021).

4 "Anxiety Disorders," World Health Organization, September 27, 2023, https://www.who.int/news-room/fact-sheets/detail/anxiety-disorders.

5 Mary Pipher, *Women Rowing North: Navigating Life's Currents and Flourishing as We Age* (New York: Bloomsbury, 2019).

6 Christine Valters Paintner, *Birthing the Holy: Wisdom from Mary to Nurture Creativity and Renewal* (Notre Dame, IN: Sorin Books, 2022) 88, xix.

7 Gary Chapman, *The Five Love Languages* (Chicago: Northfield Publishing, 1995).

8 See chapter 5 in Wendy M. Wright, *Seasons of a Family's Life: Cultivating the Contemplative Spirit at Home* (San Francisco: Jossey-Bass, 2011).

The Authors

SHERAH-LEIGH GERBER is a spiritual director and caregiver coach in northeastern Ohio. She is an ordained minister in Mennonite Church USA, and she holds a master of divinity degree. Sherah-Leigh has served as a pastor in addition to working in other nonprofit leadership roles. She lives with her husband and two middle school–aged children on a fifth-generation farm, which provides many opportunities to find the sacred in the ordinary. You can learn more about her work at SherGerber.com.

GWEN LANTZ holds several jobs, including bookkeeper, elementary school librarian, and writer. She has a master's degree in education with a specialty in school library science. Gwen lives with her husband and two children in the Shenandoah Valley of Virginia and is a lifelong member of the Mennonite Church. She enjoys engaging with her church community and pursuing personal spiritual growth amid everyday life. You can see more of her writing at SomeComfortAndJoy.com.